Breaking The Spirit of POVERTY

Mark W. Pfeifer

Copyright © 2006 by Mark W. Pfeifer

All rights reserved. No part of this publication may be reproduced or transmitted in any form or by any means, electronic or mechanical, including photocopying, recording, or by any information storage and retrieval system, without written permission of the publisher.

Bible references: NEW KING JAMES VERSION
Copyright © 1982 by Thomas Nelson, Inc.

Breaking the Spirit of Poverty
By Mark W. Pfeifer

First Printing: September, 2006
Second Printing: February, 2007
Third Printing: June, 2007

ISBN 13: 978-0-9788765-0-0
ISBN 11: 0-9788765-0-4

Library of Congress Control Number: 2006907781

Published by SOMA, Inc.
P. O. Box 913
Chillicothe, Ohio 45601
(740) 703-5497

To order additional copies please contact the publisher
Order on-line at www.somafamily.com

For bookings contact Mark and Nicki Pfeifer
P. O. Box 913
Chillicothe, Ohio 45601
(740)703-5497, 5597

Printed in the United States by Morris Publishing
3212 East Highway 30
Kearney, NE 68847
1-800-650-7888

This book is lovingly dedicated to
my family…

Nicki, my love!
Andrew, my first!
Alexandra, my girl!
Austin, my bonus!

ACKNOWLEDGEMENTS

Achieving in life takes a team. Sometimes the body of Christ is an army; sometimes it is a family. Either way, generals and fathers need both soldiers and children in order to do what they do. These people identify us, support us and help us fulfill our destinies. In return, we do the best we can to serve these great people from victory to victory.

First, I want to thank my Lord, my Savior, Jesus Christ!

Running a close second is my family, my wife being the first! Nicki has always challenged me to live above mediocrity and dream big! My three children remind me that it's always worth it to press on. Their futures depend on it.

I also thank God for my brothers, sister and parents who continually give me life.

I would like to thank the staff at Open Door: Chuck, Sandy, Stan, Rhonda, Rick, Dawn, Joel and Amber. I also would like to thank the elders of Open Door: Chuck, Jim and Fred. I also give my appreciation to the many leaders who serve the great church that I pastor: Cell group leaders, deacons and other servants who have laid down their lives for the cause of Christ. The entire congregation of Open Door is an amazing group of people! It is my joy and honor to have served you these many years and I look forward to many more years to come.

My thanks goes out to the SOMA Leadership Council: Nicki, Tom, Troy and Steve. I also want to recognize all of the SOMA pastors and leaders who are standing together in order to break the spirit of poverty in their families, churches, cities and regions.

Thanks Jenny for all your hard work on this manuscript and Ron and Amanda for your time proofreading it.

TABLE OF CONTENTS

Author's Foreword 6

1. Buried Treasure 9
2. Thinking Outside the Poverty Box 20
3. The Power to Get Wealth 31
4. Pleasing God with Your Increase 44
5. Looking Through the Poverty Lens 60
6. Your Promise Needs a Blessing 73
7. Learning to Release 82
8. Farmers, Seeds and Soil 100
9. Four Types of Giving 110
10. Why Do Preachers Talk About Money All of the Time? 124
11. Keeping the Accursed Thing 134

Conclusion 143

AUTHOR'S FOREWORD

The spirit of poverty pulls a blinder over our eyes and puts fear in our hearts. It steals our ambitions and dreams. It tears us down with reminders of what we lack and makes us feel lesser than other people. In the end, the spirit of poverty will drive us to the backyard with shovel and treasure in hand. It convinces us that the greatest victory that we could ever win would be not to lose. So we dig our holes and bury our treasures.

It was a cold night in Canada. The wind swept landscape created an arctic wonderland as the thermometer dropped well below zero. Inside the sanctuary of the church where we were attending a pastor's conference, Nicki and I were being stirred. We were challenged to dream bigger dreams and move in greater faith. As is often the case with such meetings, the stirring came and the stirring went. By the time we returned home, our excitement was beginning to melt away like the winter's snow and the stirring that we had felt only a few weeks earlier was almost entirely gone.

If there is anything that I have learned since that cold night back in January of 1999, it is this: Don't wait until a convenient time to obey the Lord - obey Him immediately! If not, the devil has ample time to talk us out of our blessing. We had made a vow for a specific amount of money that we did not have in the bank at that time. We came forward during that night's service and committed ourselves that if God would supply the need, then we would sow the seed. I remember the weeks going by and then one day I went to the mailbox. There in my possession was a check for a little over the amount that we had pledged! As I walked to the house the Lord reminded me of our promise - He was not the only one that was talking that day!

I remember thinking to myself, "Wow, we could sure use this money right now. The kids need summer clothes. We need improvements on the house. It's been so long now since we made that vow that the church probably doesn't need it anymore. Besides, they have plenty of money. A lot of other people responded the night we went forward. It's no big deal. I'll get another check and pay that vow later."

Fast-forward six years...

In the summer of 2005 Nicki was sensing like the Lord wanted to break a spirit of poverty off of our church and over us. As she prayed, the Lord reminded her that we had not done what we promised. We had not paid our vow to that church. He further revealed to her that we, as the primary leaders of our congregation, were holding back the blessings of God from a lot of other people, as well. After six years, Nicki sat down and wrote that check along with a letter of apology to the pastors of the church. We still had plenty of other bills that needed paid but we knew that a lot was riding on our obedience.

Not long after the check left our hands, miraculous things began to happen. It was like blinders had been taken off our eyes and a lid was removed from our ministries. The church we pastor began to prosper. Not only us but also people around us began to dream bigger dreams and see greater visions. They were receiving breakthroughs that they were expecting for a long time. For us personally, within days of obeying God, major debts were erased and we received significant spiritual and financial blessings. It was hard for me to imagine what one little offering could do. It made me kick myself for not having obeyed the Lord six years earlier!

This book represents what I can now see more clearly than ever before. There is a spirit of poverty in the church that must be broken. The church has a job to do. We are called to advance the Kingdom of God around the earth. This is a major undertaking that will take big dreams, greater visions and significant wealth being transferred from the world and into the hands of the righteous. My hope and prayer is that you will join the growing number of people who are crying out and battling against the spirit of poverty. With God's help, we can reach out to families and entire communities, helping to change their destinies forever. We can promote and expand the Kingdom rule of God around the earth. Jesus said that the "gospel of the Kingdom will be preached in all the world as a witness to all nations, and then the end will come (Matthew 24:14)." The ultimate goal of this book is to help make that happen!

Mark W. Pfeifer
June 6, 2006

Chapter 1

"Buried Treasure"

The master of the estate was packed and ready to leave on his journey. He would be gone for a long time and he worried about the welfare of his estate while he was away. He sat alone in his office pondering what to do when the answer occurred to him. "I have three good managers," he said to himself, "I'll let them continue my business while I'm gone. They'll do a good job. They have always served me well."

Soon, all three managers were sitting in front of their master's desk waiting for their assignments. The first manager was a strong, industrious man from a good family. To this employee, the master of the estate gave 5,000 dollars and told him to do with it as he pleased. "When I return," the boss said with a wink, "I want to see what you have done with my money." The young man shook his hand and left the room.

The second servant was a loyal man. He had worked for this boss for several years and had proven himself on many occasions. The master opened the top drawer of his desk and handed the servant an envelope containing 2,000 dollars. The two shook hands while the envelope passed between them. The boss said, "Take this money and do with it as you see fit." With that, the faithful servant gave a nod of humble approval, turned with military precision and left the room.

③The final servant was a good man. He never stole anything. He never cheated anyone. He never made fatal mistakes. He was a safe, deliberate chap who never lost money, was never impulsive nor took many risks. He was always the first one to give warning whenever anyone stepped out into the unknown. He was always the one everyone counted on to give caution to new ideas. He had worked the longest for the master of the estate and had made a very safe and happy home for himself and his family. He was a real Steady-Eddy.

When he received his envelope, the boss made the same appeal, "Do with it as you see fit. When I return, I want to see what you did with my money." The manager waited until he had left his boss's office before opening up the envelope. There he found $1,000. The conversation that he had with himself might have gone something like this: "Only a grand? Why only 1,000 dollars? He gave those other managers more than he did me. Maybe he doesn't like me. He must have more confidence in them than he does me. He probably doesn't have any faith in me, at all. Why else would he give me less than half? He knows that I am lesser than they; that I have less ability; less education; less ingenuity. I guess I really am a nobody!"

The impoverished servant began to think about what to do with his cash. "Well, I can't give it away. It's all I have," he reasoned. "If I had 5,000 dollars like the first servant I could invest it or something. But if I let go of my money and lose it, I'll have nothing!" Fear gripped the fretful servant as he thought about losing his precious cash. What would he tell the boss? What would he say to the other managers? What would he say to his family?

As the manager mused over his decision, he remembered his master's instructions "Do with it as you see fit." He thought for a minute. Finally, an idea came to him. "I'll bury it! That will keep it safe. Nobody can take it then. It's the best that I can do. After all, I'm not very smart; not very educated; not very successful. The best that I can do is not losing what I have." With that, he found his shovel and headed for the backyard.

THE SENSE OF LACK

I want to suggest to you that this servant was operating under a spirit of poverty. What is poverty? It is a sense of lack in all things. It's the identity and self-image that controls the way that people think, see circumstances, judge reality and draw conclusions about themselves and others. It includes money but is not limited to money. It is lack in all things. People who labor under the yoke of poverty feel lesser than other people most of the time. Sometimes it compels them to overachieve while at other times the spirit of poverty causes people to underachieve. For this reason, a spirit of poverty cannot be found in what someone has received, but in what they have given away. This spirit keeps people from dreaming dreams, taking risks and releasing to others. They live in fear of losing what they have so they bury every form of treasure that they own. They have a difficult time giving away love, compliments, friendships and money.

People living under a spirit of poverty never feel strong enough to survive. They don't feel smart enough to succeed, fortunate enough to catch a break, loved enough to be secure, nice enough to have friends, prosperous enough to get ahead and wealthy enough to give to others. This sense of lack creates fear that convinces them that to bury their treasure is the safest form of security and peace. To these people, not losing is winning; not giving up ground is progress; not dying is living and not failing is success. The spirit of poverty can infect individuals, families, churches, cities and entire nations.

GOD'S WILL FOR ABUNDANCE

Christ told the above story in the 25th chapter of Matthew. Verse 14 says, "For the Kingdom of Heaven is like a man traveling into a far country who called his own servants and delivered his goods to them. And for one he gave five talents; to another two; to another one; each according to his own ability..." The next verse says, "Then he who had received the five went and traded with them and made another five."

This story tells us that the first servant who received five talents was prosperous. In this passage "talent" is not ability or gifting but a measure of money. The first man was given an amount of money and he was able to trade it to create more. When you trade something, what do you do with your possession? You give it away. When you trade, you give up what you have for something better or for something more. It's impossible to trade something unless you are willing to release it. We can see from the very beginning that the success of the first servant was found when he opened up his hand to release his wealth.

Verse 17 in the passage says, "And likewise, he who had received two gained two more." We assume that he did so by trading. These first two men were prosperous because they looked at what they had, took risks and released it for the promise of something greater. God gave them a certain allotment and they were prosperous. They multiplied it. What is amazing in this passage is that success is assured in the obedience. There was no mention of ever losing what they had been given. If they obeyed and followed the master's plan, they would succeed. Period.

God's will for you is abundance. Until you stop fighting that reality, you will constantly labor under a spirit of poverty. God's will for you is increase. "Beloved, I pray that you may prosper in all things and be in health, just as your soul prospers (III John 2)." Don't just put a dollar sign on what I just said. When I start talking about poverty and prosperity, you cannot hear the term "money" alone. It is a greater issue than finances. God wants you to increase and be prosperous in every area of your life - mentally, spiritually, financially, relationally, etc. The Bible is full of promises for increase. It's full of direction. It's full of principles, which if applied, will bring multiplication. God is a God of abundance and His will for you is to succeed.

If there is something that rises up in you that wants to say "yes-but," what is rising up in you is a spirit of poverty. If something rises up in you that says, "Oh, but not me," that is a spirit of poverty. It will argue against the truth of God's word.

A spirit of poverty gives you a sense of lack in every area of your life. It includes money, but is not limited to that. You feel a lack when it comes to spiritual power. You feel as bankrupt spiritually as you do financially. When it comes to love, you feel a sense of emptiness, a sense of lack. When someone talks about you being more than a conqueror and when people say that you are blessed, that spirit of poverty says, "No you're not! That is for somebody else but not you." Because of a spirit of poverty you may have a hard time believing that you are fully blessed, totally victorious and completely able to prosper.

The spirit of poverty has robbed God's people so deeply of His blessings that we have come to expect lack in our families and congregations. We think that it's normal not to have enough. We think that it's normal to be in debt over our heads and unable to fulfill the vision of the church because there are insufficient funds. I want to tell you that there is an abundance of funds available. The problem is a spirit of poverty. It has convinced us to bury our treasure out of fear instead of releasing it in faith. It has, therefore, depleted us from walking in the fullness of God. Any economist will tell you that nations suffer not because of a lack of funds but because of a lack of releasing those funds into the marketplace. Wealth is to be distributed not withheld. It's a spirit of poverty that has kept us from releasing what we have in order to keep us from walking in God's abundance and prosperity.

Don't ever forget that the multitudes were fed because of a little boy who broke a spirit of poverty by releasing what he had. Until we learn to release what we have been given, the spirit of poverty will continue to rob the church blind and keep our families living in lack for generations to come. We are like the servant who buried what he had been given out of fear and insecurity.

➔ POVERTY IS NOT A BLESSING FROM GOD

Many of us have grown up under a spirit of poverty. We have been led to believe that more government handouts are the answer. In fact, the spirit of poverty wants to convince people that they have so much lack in their lives that they can never succeed on their own. They are convinced that they need "Big Brother" to help them. Thus, the welfare roles increase and the entitlement society is perpetuated from generation to generation. They feel helpless, hopeless and in despair.

If you hear yourself saying things like, "I could never do that," or, "I'm not smart enough," or "Good things never happen to me," or "I could never be that successful." That's a spirit of poverty speaking. It zeros in on your sense of lack and makes you stop believing in yourself. If you don't believe in yourself, no one will ever believe in you. This kind of debilitating and humiliating attitude is not what God had in mind when He created Adam and Eve.

Nowhere in the Bible does it say that poverty is a blessing. There is not one scripture in the Bible that says, "And God blessed his covenant people with a great blessing of poverty from generation to generation." Nowhere in the Bible does it say, "And God rewarded his people with great poverty." In fact, the Bible is very clear that poverty is not a blessing from God. When you look at poverty, there is no redeeming value in it. <u>We have this misconception sometimes in the church that poverty equals humility. All that poverty and humility have in common is that a spirit of poverty will humiliate you!</u> That's the only connection that can be made. Nowhere in the Bible does it talk about poverty being a blessing for God's children.

When you look around the world and you see poverty, what do you see? You tell me. You will see drug addiction, sickness, depression, suicide, broken relationships, incest, sexual perversion, pregnancies outside of wedlock and children being raised without parents, etc. If poverty equals piety and is a great spiritual blessing of God, then the greatest revivals on the planet are happening in the ghettos and slums right now. It ought to be the goal of every spiritual Christian, then, to starve their children and live in lack. That's ludicrous, isn't it? It's just as preposterous to believe that poverty is somehow a redeeming factor for mankind. How can we help the poor if we are all poor? How can we feed the hungry if we have no extra food? How can we cloth the naked if we have no extra clothes? Someone in the church had better prosper and learn how to release what they have been given in order to fulfill the commandment to help those in need.

Now maybe you want to say to me, "Oh, Pastor Mark, the Bible says the love of money is the root of all evil!" I would say to you that the love of anything besides God is the root of all kinds of evil. It is not what you have that matters; it's what you love. True, the love of money is the root of all kinds of evil. However, we are not talking about the love of money here. We are talking about the love of what a person can do with their money by advancing the Kingdom of God and helping humanity. It ought to be the goal of every Christian to have more than enough so that they can give generously to those who need it. The prospect of releasing thousands, if not millions, of dollars into the Kingdom of God worldwide ought to excite every true believer. If it doesn't, then maybe you should check what it is that you truly love!

The spirit of poverty operates so deeply in people, convincing them of their lack, that they fill their lives with all kinds of illegitimate things. This gnawing sense of lack drives them to try and numb the pain and fill the void with all kinds of unhealthy and harmful things. Growing up in Southern Ohio I have seen firsthand what a spirit of poverty can do. One of the things you will find in places where there is a strong spirit of poverty is a high percentage of obesity, addictions and disease. People are constantly trying to fill their sense of lack with harmful and even deadly things. These humiliating conditions abound where there is a concentration of poverty. In Southern Ohio, for instance, the percentages of drug addiction, alcoholism, teen pregnancy and child abuse are higher than in other parts of the state. Why? Because of the spirit of poverty!

The spirit of poverty creates such a sense of lack internally that people try to fill it any way they can, whether it is a whole box of Twinkies or a whole carton of cigarettes or a whole case of beer or a fifth of whiskey. Moving from one relationship with a man to another, women and little girls, under the influence of a spirit of poverty, will offer up their virginity on the altar of poverty just to hear a guy say, "I love you." Why? They are trying to fill that internal sense of lack that resides within them. The spirit of poverty has robbed them.

THE DEADLY TRINITY

To the first two servants that released what they had been given and experienced multiplication and abundance, Jesus said, "Well done my good and faithful servant." These two men operated from a spirit of success and prosperity. They were doing the will of God. They had foresight and vision. They wanted to make more money and do greater things. They saw that prosperity was pleasing to their Master. They saw it as their work for God. They didn't see poverty as a blessing from God and prosperity as an evil curse. Those guys had an attitude of increase and God rewarded it!

The spirit of poverty was operating on the third guy. What did he do? "But he who had received one went and dug in the ground, and hid his Lord's money (Matthew 25:18)." Why did he do that? Skip down to Verse 24 and 25 for the answer. "He who had received one talent came and said, 'Lord, I knew you to be a hard man, reaping where you have not sown and gathering where you had not scattered seed. I was afraid and I hid your money." The spirit of poverty is connected with a spirit of fear and a spirit of fear is connected to a spirit of religion. I want to put those three links together for a moment: poverty, fear, and religion.

The reason that religion is connected to poverty is because religion always tells you that you are never good enough. Religion brings the standard of perfection and measures you beside it, making you feel "lesser than." This arouses and confirms the sense of lack that people already feel from the spirit of poverty. This propagates this whole feeling of emptiness and insecurity.

Wherever you find poverty, you'll always find a strong spirit of religion. Where there is a strong spirit of religion, you will always find great poverty. These two spirits are like Siamese twins. What links them both together is fear. Notice again what this man said in the passage: "And I was afraid, and went and hid your talent in the ground. (Matthew 25:25)." Let me tell you why the man was afraid. He was afraid because of the skewed condition of his self-image after the spirit of poverty had raped his self-confidence. He felt sure that he would be a failure. He felt sure that he would lose what he had been given. He felt sure that the Master would reject him. So he did what seemed logical and safe. He hid the Lord's money.

Success in this parable was assured in the effort of obedience. But this man didn't even want to try and succeed because he was afraid he might lose what he had been given. The spirit of poverty makes a person afraid to let go. They become afraid of giving. "Because if I give it away," they conclude, "I won't have anything left for me. I'll be empty." Their logic says, "It's better just to keep what I have, dig a hole and hide it than to risk losing it."

Do you see the church wrapped up in that mentality? It seems that we're so busy protecting what we have that we become afraid to move into anything new. We're busy protecting what God did a hundred years ago. We're afraid that we're going to lose our members; lose our reputation; lose our bank accounts. Acting out of fear, we do what many churches do; we circle the wagons and start burying our treasure. Never forget that the same rules that apply to individuals also apply to congregations. The first step in abundance and multiplication is to release what we have been given, not to try and hold it back.

IT'S TIME TO BREAK THE CYCLE

What we inherit from our parents becomes increased when we add it to what we have accumulated over our lifetimes. Generational blessings increase and so do generational curses. The spirit of poverty will increase with every generation unless it is broken – NOW! We must repent of walking under a poverty spirit, receive the truth of God's Word for prosperity and walk in a different mindset. We must refuse to walk in fear and religion. The battle cry of the religious is, "Let's not go too far!" I want to ask you a question: What would happen if we went too far? Aren't there enough Christians running around today that aren't going far enough that it might not be so bad to balance them out by having a few of us go "too far?"

Friend, I would rather die bankrupt having tried great things for God than succeed in burying my treasure. I don't want to have to go searching in the ground to find the last great moves of God. I don't want to have to read another man's treasure map to find the miracles of the Bible. We go digging in the past every year to find the last time the church stepped out in faith and call it "homecoming." That's when we all stand around and ooh and awe about a previous generation's release of faith while we have made costly investments in shovels.

We go searching in the pages of history and show off our Azusa Street talent; our John Wesley talent; our Lutheran talent; our Episcopalian talent. We show off our buried treasure that identifies us with great men and women of God in history and we eulogize what God did in the past. But where is our talent? What are we releasing in faith?

God is interested in you releasing and multiplying what you have. But you will never have multiplication in your life if you operate in a poverty mindset because you will always bury your talent in fear and insecurity. You are going to die with every talent that God has ever given you buried in your backyard if you operate this way. Poverty, fear and religion will go hand-in-hand-in-hand, like demonic triplets, keeping you from walking in the fullness of God.

CHAPTER 2

"Thinking Outside the Poverty Box"

Poverty drives people to bury their treasure in the backyard. This parable is literal. I know people that don't want you bringing a metal detector in their backyard. They have wealth but won't release it. They have created a world of poverty around them by viewing themselves and others through the lens of lack. They are afraid to love; afraid to hope; afraid to dream; afraid to have visions; afraid to trust God. Like a flower that is closed off, afraid of being rejected, they keep everyone in their life at arm's length.

I'm not talking about Heaven or hell issues. I'm talking about life. You will go to Heaven, but you will never reach your destiny here on earth if you walk under a spirit of poverty. You will never fulfill your purposes in God while living out of a poverty spirit.

To help us think outside the box (prison) of poverty, let's look at God's Word for a moment. The very first command that God gave to humanity was, "Be fruitful and multiply; fill the earth and subdue it; have dominion over the fish of the sea, over the birds of the air, and over every living thing that moves on the earth (Genesis 1:28)." As you can see, His intention for us all along was progress, prosperity and promotion. The devil has convinced us that we should live in poverty. Why? Because the enemy knows that in order to advance the Kingdom of God around the earth, someone will have to dream big. Someone will have to finance this worldwide endeavor. Someone will have to think outside the box, un-circle the wagons and carry on.

Proverbs 10:15 says, "The rich man's wealth is his strong city; the destruction of the poor is their poverty." In the next chapter Proverbs 11:24 says, "There is one who scatters, yet increases more; and there is one who withholds more than is right, but it leads to poverty." If you withhold and bury your wealth, it will lead to poverty but the generous soul who releases it will be made rich. Think of that!

Proverbs 28:19 says, "He who tills his land will have plenty of bread, but he who follows frivolity will have poverty enough!" Does it sound to you that the Biblical writers believed that poverty was a blessing from God? Do you suppose that they thought that to be poor and to be humble were one and the same? I don't.

I hear people make statements like this all the time: "Well, I don't need all of that prosperity stuff. All I need is enough for me and my family." Do you know what that is? That's selfishness masquerading itself in humility and spirituality. As believers, we ought to be praying that God gives us enough for our families AND enough for the neighbor down the street who lost his job AND for the church building plans AND for the missionaries AND for the food pantry AND...

Do you see what I mean?

III John 2 says, "Beloved, I pray that you may prosper in all things and be in health, just as your soul prospers." The Apostle John wanted his flock to prosper. What about Paul? He reminded the Philippians in 4:19 "God shall supply all your needs according to His riches in glory by Christ Jesus." Again, when motivating the Corinthians to release their wealth into his hands for the purpose of blessing the Jerusalem Church Paul said, "But this I say: He who sows sparingly will also reap sparingly, and he who sows bountifully will also reap bountifully. So let each one give as he purposes in his heart, not grudgingly or of necessity; for God loves a cheerful giver (II Corinthians 9:7)."

Moses established the Law for God's people and made sure that they understood their covenant blessing of prosperity when he said in Deuteronomy 8:18, "And you shall remember the LORD your God, for it is He who gives you power to get wealth, that He may establish His covenant which He swore to your fathers, as it is this day." In order to establish the covenant upon the earth and advance this great Kingdom message around the world, this poverty spirit must be broken and someone reading this book must be blessed and released to be extremely prosperous and generous with their harvest.

THE BIBLICAL WRITERS

The Jews have never had a problem seeing that poverty is not a blessing from God. They have never had a problem seeing that prosperity is part of the covenant blessing of God to his people. The Biblical writers were Jews and they understood that abundance was God's plan for his obedient children. Do you know why they believed that? Because the Bible makes bold claims like these:

> Ps. 112:1-3
>
> "Praise the LORD! Blessed is the man who fears the LORD, Who delights greatly in His commandments. His descendants will be mighty on earth; The generation of the upright will be

blessed. Wealth and riches will be in his house, And his righteousness endures forever."

Ps. 118:24-25
"This is the day the LORD has made; We will rejoice and be glad in it. Save now, I pray, O LORD; O LORD, I pray, send now prosperity."

Ps. 122:6-7
"Pray for the peace of Jerusalem: 'May they prosper who love you. Peace be within your walls, Prosperity within your palaces.'"

Mal 3:10
"Bring all the tithes into the storehouse, That there may be food in My house, And try Me now in this,' Says the LORD of hosts, 'If I will not open for you the windows of heaven And pour out for you such blessing that there will not be room enough to receive it.'"

Is. 60:5, 11
"Then you shall see and become radiant, And your heart shall swell with joy; Because the abundance of the sea shall be turned to you, The wealth of the Gentiles shall come to you… Therefore your gates shall be open continually; They shall not be shut day or night, That men may bring to you the wealth of the Gentiles, And their kings in procession."

The Jewish people had an expectation of prosperity and provision as a part of the covenant that they had with God. As

Christians, coming to God with a better covenant (Hebrews 7:22), should we expect no less? Why would God make one covenant with His people that included wealth and abundance and then make a greater covenant with them that cancelled that part of the blessing and replaced it with poverty? It doesn't make sense. Yet here we are, 2,000 years after Christ still struggling with the idea that to be poor is spiritual; to live in lack is self-denial; to barely have enough is trusting God; to be poor is pious. While at the same time we believe that to be prosperous is worldly-minded and carnal. How did we come to that conclusion?

THE ROOT OF THE POVERTY MYTH

Here is where we have got to back up in time a little bit. If the Jewish people of the Old Testament and the Christian Jews of the First Century both believed that abundance and prosperity were a part of the covenant plan of God, then where did we get the notion that to be poor was spiritual? Where did get the idea that to have no money was a sign of humility?

In order to find the answer to this question, we have to go back about 2,500 years. The Greeks were the dominant world power thanks to the bold and audacious leadership of Alexander the Great. The Greeks imputed their culture upon the people and nations that they conquered. Because of this, their way of thinking is still dominating our way of thinking in the Western world to this day.

Plato was the architect for much of Greek philosophy. His teachings influenced the way that the average Greek man, woman and child saw the world. When the Romans replaced the Greeks several generations later as the eminent power of the Mediterranean world, Plato's teachings stood the test of time and remained engrained in the Roman worldview.

Plato saw the universe as existing in two distinct forms, the spiritual world and the material world. We wouldn't say that is wrong. In fact, the Bible teaches the reality of both worlds existing together in God's created universe. However, Plato dissected the reality and roles of these two worlds so distinctly, that it gave rise to the notion that they were practically independent of one another.

In the Greek way of thinking, everything in the natural world was an imperfect shadow of its spiritual counterpart. The spiritual world was perfect, flawless, void of defect while the physical world was imperfect, flawed and full of defects. This way of thinking gave rise to a philosophy called Gnosticism. Coming from the Greek word for knowledge, this way of thinking propagated the notion that nothing good comes from the physical world. In fact, nothing holy and perfect could ever have physical properties since the material world is completely flawed to the core. Only the spirit world could contain anything with merit and worthwhile.

People who thought this way had a hard time understanding the incarnation of Christ. "If Christ came in the flesh," the Gnostic mused, "then how could He be sinless and holy?" To answer this question, the Gnostics proposed that Jesus really did not come in the flesh but was a spiritual anomaly that only appeared to be flesh and blood. He really did not come in the flesh and walk among people. He only pretended to be a human with a physical body.

This philosophy so threatened the church by the end of the First Century that John wrote several passages against such thinking. For instance, John 1:14 says, "And the Word became flesh and dwelt among us, and we beheld His glory, the glory as of the only begotten of the Father, full of grace and truth." He also said in I John 4:2-3, "By this you know the Spirit of God: Every spirit that confesses that Jesus Christ has come in the flesh is of God and every spirit that does not confess that Jesus Christ has come in the flesh is not of God. And this is the spirit of the Antichrist..."

This Platonic way of thinking splits the spiritual world from the physical world right down the middle. On one side of the line we have perfection, on the other side of the line we have imperfection. On one side of the line we have what is holy, on the other side of the line we have what is unholy. Approaching life with this duality runs right down the center of the universe splitting the spirit world from the physical world.

Unfortunately, we still do the same today. We live out of a Greek mindset, which has the same dissection between the physical world and the spiritual world. And here is how we express that belief: On Sunday we go to church and then we draw the line for the rest of the week. We have devotions to be with God, and then we have the rest of our lives to ourselves. We have separated the spiritual from the secular; the clergy from the laity; worship from work; religion from business. We see certain aspects of our lives as spiritual while other parts of our lives we see as secular, having nothing to do with God and church. We conveniently segregate our spiritual lives from our normal, everyday life. After all, church is church and business is business! Right?

The Gnostics who attended church services in Biblical times didn't come to worship wearing a T-shirt that said, "Hi, I am a Gnostic." They didn't wear buttons or have Gnostic bumper stickers. They didn't even think about it. It seemed to be a natural and perfectly normal perspective of life. But yet this philosophy influenced them. They understood the physical world as being imperfect with an ugly, horrible and sinful nature while the only good and perfect existence in the universe was in the spiritual world.

Armed with this worldview, the Gnostics developed a way of thinking with which we are still battling today. It goes something like this: "If it feels good, it can't be Godly." We may also express it like this: "If it feels good, it should be avoided." How many people have heard preaching that way? This world is dirty and sinful and horrible. How dare you enjoy something entertaining? How dare you laugh? How dare you enjoy the things of this world? A person can get the idea that being spiritual means avoiding joy in life at all costs.

The Jews never struggled with this kind of worldview. They believed like Paul when he told Timothy in I Timothy 6:17 that God has given us "all things to enjoy." They understood what the Psalmist meant in 24:1 when he declared that the earth is the Lord's and all of its fullness. The Jews had no Platonic understanding of the dissection of the universe with its spiritual world and the physical world being unrelated. To them, it was all good and holy because God created it. Therefore, to enjoy the physical sensations and material blessings of the earth were just as holy as experiencing the spiritual blessing that comes from the presence of the Lord. It was all Godly and meant for humanity to experience with great joy.

Let me give you an illustration. It is impossible for you to fully separate your brain from your mind. Correct? How do you separate your brain from your mind? If you have brain damage, it affects your mind. If you have problems with your mind, it will affect the electrical impulses of your brain. They are interconnected. Your mind and your brain cannot be dissected because they are defined by one another. They interact with one another. They are intertwined with one another.

So it is with the physical world and the spiritual world. They are intertwined with one another, both affecting one another. The Jews understood that there is no clear line of demarcation between the

BREAKING THE SPIRIT OF POVERTY

spiritual world and the material world. Perfect or imperfect, it was all created by God to bless mankind. That's why He made every human being with the capacity to experience both worlds simultaneously.

You ask, "Mark, what does that have to do with poverty?" I'll tell you how. In 313, Constantine was converted and he made Christianity the Imperial religion of the Roman Empire. They were Greek thinkers. For the next 1,000 years, the Church was no longer influenced by the Jewish way of thinking but it was dominated by the Greek way of thinking. It was during this time that Gnosticism began to influence Church policy with greater success. During the Middle Ages the Church came up with this idea that if it feels good, it must be wrong. If it feels good, it's sinful.

Consequently, in order to be a priest and wholly dedicated to God, a person had to take certain vows. One was a vow of celibacy. To this day the Roman Catholic priests do not marry because of this Gnostic way of thinking that says, "If it feels good, it is wrong." Sex couldn't possibly be good for you. It's too physical and feels too good.

Have you ever thought about the fact that God invented sex? It was His idea. He created a man and a woman and gave them the ability to become one flesh. Through sexual intercourse, God gave humanity the ability to operate in such a covenant that they become inseparably unified both physically and spiritually. He also created them to have sex strictly for enjoyment.

The Jews had no problem understanding that sex was a gift from God. In fact, in order to be on the Sanhedrin and to be a Pharisee, you had to be married. The Old Testament talks about the blessing of having a full quiver, meaning many children. That means a lot of sex!

There is another vow the priest took. That was a vow of poverty. What I want to suggest to you is the vow of poverty and the vow of celibacy were both linked, not to the Bible, but to Gnosticism. It was birthed from Greek philosophies that said that there is a separation between the spiritual world and the physical world, and anything in the physical world that feels good to our physical bodies is wrong and sinful.

It's interesting that Protestants have dealt with the celibacy issue but we're still holding to the vow of poverty. When you were saved, you didn't take a vow of poverty. Poverty is not a blessing from God. It is a curse. Just as surely as procreating the human race is an act of obedience in order to be fruitful and multiply, it is also a command that is to be applied to areas of finance and influence. Being fruitful and multiplying, subduing the earth and taking dominion is also a financial, relational, personal, intellectual and spiritual commission.

Our forefathers in the church have unfortunately sold us out with the vow of poverty that somehow portrays poverty as being humble. We are still suffering the consequences of living under that false notion. It didn't come from the Bible. It came from ancient Greek philosophy.

WHO SHOULD PROSPER AND WHO SHOULD NOT

When my father was a young, impressionable preacher, he asked an old Methodist minister why he wore threadbare suits with worn out elbows and knees. He said, "Brother Pfeifer, when you are in ministry, you can't dress real nice. If you wear new suits, people will think that you're rich and they won't give into the offering." Can you imagine that? I can! That kind of thinking has been in the church for centuries and is still alive and well today. It even means more than the suit that a man or woman of God wears, it also includes the car he or she drives, the home they live in and the accessories they wear with the new suit!

There are very few people in our society that receive more criticism for being blessed then preachers receive. Prosperity is O.K. for the athlete, the banker, the business owner, the salesman, the marketer, the actor, the singer, the doctor and the lawyer but not for the preacher! People regularly pay $20 a ticket to go watch a great athlete play sports and hope and pray everyday for their kids to play just like him. We pay $90.00 a month for our cable package to watch the NCAA championship, the NFL and NASCAR without ever thinking that our participation as fans pays their million dollar salaries. We don't think a thing about how we contribute to the salaries of actors when we are watching TV and sitting through all of the commercials. We don't think anything about paying the salaries of movie stars when we are purchasing our movie tickets or buying our popcorn and soda pop. But let the man or woman of God make more money than us and we snarl! Not many people stop watching their favorite sports team or stop watching television because of the abundance of wealth generated by athletes and actors but the devil has talked many people into leaving churches because of the financial blessings that God has given to His servants behind the pulpit. What a shame!

It's time to understand that poverty is not a sign of spirituality. It's not your job or mine to make sure that pastors remain humble by keeping them and their families in lack. In fact, the minister ought to be a leading example in all things. Instead of pointing our children towards the examples of the rich and famous movie actors and athletes, how about pointing them towards the anointed and highly successful men and women of God? I wonder what that would do for our families and for the church if we did.

CHAPTER 3

"The Power to Get Wealth"

Deuteronomy 8:18 says, "And you shall remember the LORD your God, for it is He who gives you power to get wealth, that He may establish His covenant which He swore to your fathers, as it is this day." Notice that it does not say that God simply gives you wealth. It says that He will give you the power to get wealth. Everything that you need to be successful and prosperous is available. The Bible gives us recipes on increase and multiplication. It teaches us how to live life and enjoy it to the max. It is the blueprint for mankind. In it you will find time-tested principles on how to win friends and influence people, how to be industrious, work hard, raise your kids, create wealth and have generational increase.

A poverty mentality steals the power to get wealth. Poverty will keep you from getting your education, finding a good job, meeting the right people, having ambition, dreaming dreams, finding a purpose, maintaining hope and having a solid marriage. The spirit of poverty will destroy you. It will make you feel like you can never succeed. It will convince you that God is angry with you most of the time. It will convince you that you are a loser and life will treat you unfairly. When opportunities do present themselves, even if you have enough faith in yourself to take advantage of it, the poverty mindset will put a paralyzing fear of failure on you that makes you shrink back from opportunities and make excuses for your inaction.

THE LID IS ON YOUR LIFE

The spirit of poverty places a lid on your life. That lid is an imaginary ceiling that says, "You can go no higher than this." It keeps us from receiving anything from above and makes us incapable of giving anything out. People who labor under a poverty mindset cannot give or receive very much. The flow of life, for all practical purposes, is stopped up by this mindset of lack.

Whether or not we can take a compliment is a good indicator of whether or not we operate in a spirit of poverty. A poverty mindset is the reason why many of us can't receive compliments. The lid is always there. When someone pays you a compliment and says, "Man, you did a great job." Your response might be, "Oh, no, I didn't." Although you so desperately want to be noticed and complimented, that spirit of poverty steals your blessing. It is always there to remind you of your lack and, with the help of a spirit of religion, your unworthiness. So for the sake of remaining "humble," you deny yourself the satisfaction of being recognized. You reject the compliment and yet yearn for it at the same time.

Do you see that in yourself? You so desire to get affirmed but when someone does it, you can't receive it. Someone says, "Boy, that was a good song" and your reaction is, "I know a lot of people that could have done better than me."

"Wow, that was a great teaching."

"Oh, well, no, it wasn't that great."

"Oh, man, thank you. That is so thoughtful that you gave me

that card."

"Oh, I'm sure a lot of people give you cards."

A spirit of poverty wants to keep you empty and unable to receive anything that would bless your life. God wants to pour out heaven all over your life but the lid is kept firmly in place by a poverty mindset and a spirit of religion that has given you a perverted definition of humility. This way, people remain isolated, disconnect from others who can help them. Their lives remain an empty field full of dirt mounds where all of our treasures have been buried. These treasures are doing the Kingdom of God no good by lying dormant beneath the lid of poverty.

The reason why I said that you couldn't receive God's blessings if you can't receive a compliment is because all of God's blessings are complimentary. We do not and cannot earn any of them. Yet we must put ourselves in a position to receive them in faith or we shall live empty lives. How can we do this? By understand that God loves us and desires to bless and prosper us.

When Nicki and I stay in a hotel, she always loads up with those little bottles of shampoo, lotion and bars of soap. I'll say, "Nicki, you are stealing." She'll says, "No, it's complimentary!"

"Oh, Nicki, we shouldn't take that."

"Why not? The price has been paid."

This illustrates how a person can operate in a spirit of poverty. While Nicki understands that these gifts are complimentary and the price has been paid in full, I will not take advantage of these things because I don't feel worthy to receive it.

In order to be fruitful and multiply, we have to allow ourselves to believe that God loves us and wants to bless us. We have to believe that Christ paid the price at Calvary to return us to our original state as people of heavenly AND earthly dominion and blessing. We have to dare to believe in ourselves. We have been filled with the Holy Spirit and have the Word of God at our fingertips to help guide us into a lifestyle that glorifies God with increase and generosity.

The Bible says in Ephesians 1:3 that "you have been blessed with every spiritual blessing in Christ Jesus." You have got to learn to receive in order to be a blessing. You have to take the lid off of your life so that the flow of God's generosity can come into you and then flow from you. God wants to use you to generate wealth for a greater purpose than yourself. If He can instill faith and generosity in you, then the windows of heaven will be open over your life and you will be a conduit to bring the blessings of heaven down to earth.

The prophets saw a transfer of wealth from the world into the hands of God's covenant people. Isaiah said in 60:5, "The wealth of the Gentiles shall come to you" and again in verse 11, "That men may bring to you the wealth of the Gentiles." Unless you know how to receive, you can never be involved in this process. Proverbs 13:22 says, "...but the wealth of the sinner is stored up for the righteous." God wants to raise up men and women who have an open hand in order to receive His blessings and an open heart in order to pass them on. These people know how to take the wealth of the world and transfer it into the hands of those who are advancing the Kingdom of God.

GENERATIONAL PROSPERITY

Prosperity simply means increase. The wonderful thing about the Bible is that it never defines what being rich means. It never does put a dollar figure on how much money it takes to be qualified as rich. I once heard someone define rich as, "Anyone that has more than me." This may be the way many people think but it's not what the Bible says. Scriptures teach that being prosperous begins with God, continues with self, extends to the family and ends with brotherly kindness. The Bible includes prosperity into every sphere. Does it mean money? Yes, but it includes more than money. God wants to increase the measure of your joy, peace, love, health, relationships, family, children, marriage, everything. All of it can come under God's blessing of increase.

My family has been prosperous. I could take you down into Pike County, Ohio, out Route 220 West, up Fish and Game Road, right up to the original Pfeifer farm where my great-great grandfather settled in 1856. We have his request for immigration papers from Germany and his citizenship papers when he came to the United States of America. He came to this country and started tilling a little hillside farm full of clay and rocks on the top of a small mountain, a place that can hardly grow grass, let alone crops. I can show you his grave overlooking the fields and forests of that small farm. I can tell you the stories of both my grandfathers singing the songs of heaven in churches large and small for over forty years. I can show you the blessings of my fore parents both materially and spiritually. I can show you businesses that they've owned, positions they have filled and thousands of people they have blessed. I can tell you about my father's ministry since 1949 and about my siblings ministering all over the United States and Canada. The generations born to that German immigrant have been prosperous because they have worked hard and God has blessed them.

The Bible gives you power to get wealth because it tells you how to work, have a good attitude, be industrious, expect good things, get an education and how to treat people. The Bible reveals all of the secrets of success whether in the church or in the world. The Bible gives you principles on how to make your life better. God wants you, right now, to determine that you will no longer walk under a poverty mentality and begin walking without the imaginary lid on your life. He wants you to determine that you and your descendants will be blessed for generations to come.

Psalm 122:1-2 declares, "Blessed is the man who fears the LORD, Who delights greatly in His commandments. His descendants will be mighty on earth; the generation of the upright will be blessed." That verse reveals God's will for you and your family.

Does it mean money? Yeah, but it means more than money. It means you can prosper in self-esteem, in your mental health, your emotional health, your body and your family. Why wouldn't everyone want that?

W-O-R-K, A FOUR LETTER WORD

Ecclesiastics 5:18 says, "It is good and fitting for one to eat and drink, and to enjoy the good of all his labor in which he toils under the sun all the days of his life which God gives him; for it is his heritage." Look at that word, labor. This verse assumes that wealth is generated and prosperity is achieved by working hard. Anyone who does not learn how to work hard and dedicate himself or herself to the task of accumulating wealth will not walk in prosperity. Accumulation means that you build up a fortune over time. You spend your money with wisdom, give offerings liberally, pay your bills and stay away from unnecessary debt. Over time, these principles will work to accumulate wealth and prosperity. Success will become more than a dream to you.

Some people are looking for the big payday. Instead of patiently accumulating wealth with hard work, they take a weekly trip to the corner market to pick some numbers in the lottery. The people who can least afford to waste their money are usually the ones that play the most. These folks are operating out of a spirit of poverty that is continuously robbing them of wealth. Here's why: They lack the self-confidence enough to believe that they can be blessed by living according to God's Word. Rather, they believe in their hearts that the only way they can be prosperous is if somebody else gives it to them. This is what keeps millions of people coming back to the lottery and millions of others plotting crimes of theft, selling drugs for a quick profit and continuing generation after generation on the welfare roles.

One of the richest men that ever lived was Solomon and he wrote in Ecclesiastes 5:19, "As for every man to whom God has given riches and wealth, and given him power to eat of it, to receive his heritage and rejoice in his labor-this is the gift of God." To be able to labor and to be successful in your work is a gift from God. If you are a ditch digger you can say, "You know, I accomplished something today and that's the best ditch that I could ever dig." To stand back and see your labor and feel successful and significant in life is a beautiful thing. You can know that you have accomplished something and rejoice in that labor at the end of the day. God wants you to experience success. He wants you to increase and be blessed. Like Solomon said, this is a gift from God.

The power to get wealth means that God will give you ambition, strategy, opportunity and encouragement. He will send you mentors and teachers to help you develop skills. He will show you good ground into which you can plant your financial seed and walk with confidence for increase.

God wants to make your life significant. Success doesn't always equal significance. What you are looking for in life is not really success but significance. Significance is found when you understand that your success can benefit others. You can be a significant person on the earth. You can help transfer wealth from the world's system and release it to help advance the Kingdom of God around the earth. It's time for us to quit saying, "Boy, I wish I could give $10,000 to missionaries" or "I wish that I could be a blessing to somebody." It's time to quit saying "I wish" and it's time to say, "I will!" We need to pray for prosperity, believe for prosperity, work for prosperity, receive prosperity and release prosperity.

Someone once told me, "Pastor, you need a vision too big for the tithes of the people to pay for." Pastors and leaders in the church need to get a grand vision from God and begin to pray that God will raise up and prosper millionaires who understand that God is blessing them to help finance Kingdom visions. I am dreaming such dreams and praying for such people. Jesus said that the Gospel of the Kingdom would be preached around the world before His return. Someone is going to have to pay for that worldwide enterprise. Like the Book of Acts shows, people will create wealth by selling lands and bring the proceeds to the apostle's feet (Acts 4:35). This is why the prophets foresaw a transfer of wealth from the world and into the Kingdom of God. This is why God wants to bless and prosper you.

I talked to a pastor the other day that has a man in his church that tithes a thousand dollars a week. He called up the pastor and said, "God is blessing my business and is going to bless it more, so starting next Sunday I'm going to double my tithe." He is giving his church $2,000 a week. His goal in life is to live off of the 10% and give away the 90%. Another friend of mine told me of a man in a church in Louisiana who owned his own business and invented a device for scaffolding. He patented his invention and sold it for a great profit. He came in to his pastor's office and he said, "Pastor, I got my first paycheck for my invention. Here is my first tithe check." The pastor opened up the envelope and there was a check for $400,000! Another pastor in Maryland tells the story of a young man who came into his office wanting prayer. He had invented an electronic device of some sort and wanted the pastor to agree with him in prayer for a certain electronic chain of stores to purchase his idea. He was on his way to the meeting that day. They prayed together, the meeting took place and the national retailer requested thousands of these little devices to put into all their stores east of the Mississippi River. This young inventor became a millionaire and began to finance his pastor's dreams and visions for their city and around the world.

Would you like to be this kind of person? Then don't wait for the big payday. Begin your journey of prosperity today by giving what you can right now. Until you learn to give at your present income level, don't expect God to give you anymore than what you already have.

10 BIBLICAL PRINCIPLES FOR INCREASE

Let me conclude this chapter with ten principles that will help you increase and generate wealth for the Kingdom of God. They are simple and practical.

(1) Be generous

You need to be a generous person. Give of your time, talents and treasure. Help everybody you can in whatever way you can as often as you can. All of this will come back to bless you. If you are not giving at 10% of your income to the church now, you cannot claim the promises of God to bless and prosper your life. The Bible teaches that the first 10% is the "tithe" and belongs to the Lord. If you keep it for yourself, in the Bible, the prophet Malachi calls you a <u>thief</u> and <u>God will not bless a thief with increase</u>. Start giving your tithes and offerings now! This is the seed that will grow into a harvest over time.

(2) Use wisdom in spending

Ask God to show you where you can get a better deal. It is not wrong to look nice, it is not wrong to have nice things, just ask God to show you where to get it without spending a lot of money. And He will! I've seen this for years. People who tithe their income are incredible shoppers. It's not because they have to, it is because God just blesses them that way. I see some of the stuff my wife has on and I am like "Wow, Nicki, that is awesome! How much did that cost me?" She'll say, "It was right there on the clearance rack, five bucks. It's just my size." It happens all the time. She is an incredibly blessed person and you can be just as blessed as her.

If at all possible, stay out of credit card debt. If you cannot afford to pay cash, walk away. Keep working hard to accumulate wealth and return when you can pay for it. There is no need taking your wealth and turning it over to the credit card companies unnecessarily.

(3) Work hard and be productive

Working with purpose and determination is a key principle of prosperity. Believe it or not, people that get blessed did something for God to bless. They worked hard. When asked about the secret of their success they may want to appear humble and say something like, "Well, it's all a blessing from God." It is that, but there is more. They didn't accumulate wealth by watching TV and lying in bed until 11:00 a.m. They worked hard and were industrious. They looked for opportunities and took advantage of them when presented. They proved themselves trustworthy by being great employees and creating happy customers. You need to do the same.

(4) Invest in yourself

If you are not willing to invest in yourself, don't ever expect anyone else to want to invest in you. You need to invest in yourself by reading books, asking for advice, getting an education and going to seminars. Investing in yourself also means to take a bath, wear some nice clothes, comb your hair and shave when you leave the house. If a person doesn't think enough about themselves to keep themselves well groomed, then no one else is going to think much about them, either.

I walked in the store the other day and spoke to a man who said sarcastically, "I got one of your mailers inviting me to your school of ministry." I said, "Really?" He then made a comment about how he couldn't come because the tuition was too high, although it's about the same price you would expect to pay for a large pizza once a week. I asked, "Don't you think that you are worth it?" Investing in yourself is the first step of inviting others to invest in you. You are the most valuable commodity that you have. Take care of yourself!

(5) Network relationships

You've heard it said that it's not what you know but whom you know that counts. It's true. I have met people who, with a single conversation, have changed my life forever. I have made friends with people who have connected me to other key people who are helping us do the work of the Kingdom of God. You need to meet those types of people, also.

If you want to prosper, be nice to people, be friends with people. You say I don't have any friends. That's not their fault, that's your fault. If you don't have any friends, that's not anybody's fault but your own. There are people out there ready and waiting to meet you and be a significant relationship in your life. Your success will depend largely upon these people and others with whom you choose to associate yourself.

(6) Hang out with successful people

The Bible says in I Corinthians 15:33 that "evil company corrupts good habits." Find people who have what you want and hang out with them. Serve them. Ask questions. Volunteer to drive them somewhere. Ask to carry their luggage. Elisha got what Elijah had by serving him. When Elijah offered his mantle, Elisha fixed a meal for both of them and began to follow Elijah. Even when the old prophet said, "Get lost, Elisha!" he kept following him. At the end of his journey, the apprentice prophet received a double portion of Elijah's anointing. Not bad!

I have found that most successful people are more than willing to share their secrets with others who are hungry to achieve similar things. But they won't invest in people who are lazy, unkempt, arrogant or untrustworthy. Prove to them that you are dedicated and loyal to them and their vision. Become an Elisha and serve them so you can receive from them.

(7) Keep your eyes focused forward

The only thing that is harder than starting is finishing. We have to think ahead and be patient until we finish. Don't give up, give in or give out. Set your face towards freedom from a poverty mindset and work towards living in the blessings of God for you and your family. You need to be dreaming bigger dreams and seeing greater visions. Don't limit yourself by staying contained under your poverty lid.

(8) Create a plan and have a strategy

What separates a vision from a fantasy is strategy! Creating a plan to achieve what you have just dreamed is vital. A strategy is a result of answering a one-word question in relation to your dream, "How?" How are you going to make it happen? How? You cannot just dream a big dream and then say, "Well, I don't know how it's going to happen. God will just have to do it." Yes, God will do it – by giving you a strategy! When God wanted a covenant people, He gave Abraham a strategy. When God wanted a nation, He gave Moses a strategy. When God wanted to give Israel victory, He gave Joshua a strategy. When God wanted His people to worship Him, He gave David a strategy. When God wanted to provide a temple for His children, He gave Solomon a strategy. When Jesus sent out the 70 disciples, He gave them a strategy. When He wanted to birth the Church, He gave the Apostles a strategy. You need a strategy!

(9) Don't be afraid to take risks

Faith necessitates risk. You cannot play it safe all of your life and operate in faith. You must learn to move at the command of God, no matter what it may look like. God rewards a person of faith and Hebrews 11:6 says that it is impossible to please God without it. Your church, ministry or business can be lead by the Holy Spirit and blessed abundantly by having leaders who take risks and step out in faith.

(10) Start now

Don't wait until some magical event takes place before you get started on your journey of increase and your freedom from the spirit of poverty. Begin to dream your dream. See your destiny. Plan your strategy right now. We've wasted enough time, haven't we?

CHAPTER 4

"Pleasing God with Your Increase"

In the parable of Matthew 25:14-20 there is a surprising fact. When the Master of the estate left, he gave His servants very few instructions on what to do with the money he gave them. They were pretty much on their own. The master left his fortune in their hands to do with it what they saw fit. When he came back, however, it's another story all together.

Upon arrival, the Master summoned His three managers into His office. The man who had been given the most came in first. He had been given $5,000 and had increased his wealth to $10,000. He made money. He was successful. He was prosperous. He had initiative. He had good ideas. He was creative. He went out in the world and worked hard. He was industrious. And the master was pleased. He said to him in verse 21, "Well done, good and faithful servant; you were faithful over a few things, I will make you ruler over many things. Enter into the joy of your Lord."

The second manager had originally received $2,000. He believed in prosperity and worked hard for increase. The Bible says that he went out and he released what he had, trading and making deals. He also was hardworking, creative and industrious. Like the first; he came back and had doubled the $2,000 and now he had $4,000. To this man the master said in verse 23, "Well done, good and faithful servant; you have been faithful over a few things, I will make you ruler over many things. Enter into the joy of your Lord."

I want you to see that this kind of effort is what pleases God. Of all of the illustrations that Jesus could have used to describe what judgment day will look like, He used a parable of prosperity to show us what God expects. Increase and multiplication are Kingdom commands. They will be part of the criteria on judgment day. Prosperity pleases God. The first two men made a lot of money and God liked it! This is not to say that the poor will not enter Heaven. But it is to say that all of us are expected to do the most that we can with what we have to advance the Kingdom of God. The people who are active, industrious, ambitious, prosperous and faithful are pleasing to the Lord. In the parable, the guys that created wealth pleased the Lord. But what about the last guy? What happens to people who are motivated by a spirit of poverty all of their lives?

The final servant entered the room. His boots were still caked with mud and his trousers were dirty at the knees. No, he had not been praying. He had been digging. He approached the Master of the estate with trembling hands. He had gladly taken his master's money but now he was trembling when he heard that Master say, "Come forth..."

Perhaps upon receiving his share of the money, he looked at the other two servants and said something like, "Well, if the man that got $5,000 loses one, he still has four. If guy that got $2,000 loses one, he still has one. But if I lose one, I'll have nothing!" Perhaps he continued, "The Master must love them more than me. I am just a nobody. I'm just a poor boy. The best thing that I can do is to bury my talent so at least I don't lose it."

The spirit of poverty infects individual believers, entire congregations, whole cities and even nations of the earth like this. It infects them with an attitude that believes not losing is winning; not giving up ground is taking ground; not being defeated is victorious; not dying is living. This is why when you ask people how their church is doing, they will often give you an answer like this: "Boy, we're doing great. We haven't lost anybody this year. We're running the same amount that we did last year, praise God!"

Where do you find that in the Bible? A spirit of poverty will rob you of your vision. A spirit of poverty will rob you of your dream. A spirit of poverty will rob you of success. It will give you a feeling that you're going to lose what you have, and the best thing that you can do is to shut off the backyard from visitors, invest in some jars and bury everything that God gave you. That becomes the surest way not to lose what we have been given. People like this live and die never having achieved a thing. What happens after you die? Hebrews 9:27 says after death comes judgment.

That's what's taking place here in Matthew Chapter 25. The entire chapter is a long discourse about the final judgment. As amazing as it may sound, it was the men who went out and made money that pleased God the most. That may surprise many of us who have been subject to a spirit of poverty because in the church, we often think the opposite. Our poverty mindset makes us look at wealthy people with distrust and disdain. The man who buried his money and did not create more wealth displeased God. Look what He says in verse 26, "You wicked and lazy servant."

Can you imagine somebody who had a spirit of poverty and was in that condition hearing those same words from the preacher? What would your reaction be to a man or woman of God calling someone a "wicked and lazy servant?" How many people would we offend if we called them that name? Yet if he or she did, they would be agreeing with the Word of God! This is what the scripture says about the man who operates out of a spirit of poverty instead of being motivated to become prosperous in order to help finance the advancement of the Kingdom of God: "Wicked and lazy!" This is what God calls the man or woman who stops dreaming dreams, seeing visions, working hard, risking in faith and being prosperous. God continues His chastening in verse 26 saying, "You knew that I reap where I have not sewn and gather where I have not scattered, so you ought to have at least deposited my money with the bankers and at my coming I would have received it back with interest."

Can you see that God expects increase?

THE ORIGINAL KINGDOM COMMAND

God told Adam and Eve in the Garden of Eden that He expected them to "Be fruitful and multiply; fill the earth and subdue it; have dominion over the fish of the sea, over the birds of the air, and over every living thing that moves on the earth (Genesis 1:28)." The original command for the Kingdom of God was subdue the earth and take dominion. God's intention for Adam was to take care of his garden paradise (Genesis 2:15). Adam and Eve didn't lie around in hammocks all day eating bon-bons and watching television. They actually worked. God's intention was to start them out in the Garden of Eden and then expand their rule over the entire earth. Now that's increase! God wanted them to prosper. He wanted them to be fruitful and multiply in all things and expand the Kingdom of God over the entire planet.

This Kingdom command is still with us today. Jesus told His disciples in Matthew 28:18-20 that, "All authority has been given to

Me in heaven and on earth. Go therefore and make disciples of all the nations, baptizing them in the name of the Father and of the Son and of the Holy Spirit, teaching them to observe all things that I have commanded you; and lo, I am with you always, even to the end of the age." Do you realize that the Kingdom of God is supposed to be expanding, increasing, prospering and multiplying? The original command of God for his Kingdom that He gave to the first Adam in the Garden of Eden is the same command that the Last Adam (Jesus Christ) gave to us. God wants increase. He has commanded it, He desires it and He expects it.

Prosperity, therefore, is not an option. It is a necessity. It should represent the norm for all believers who are truly Kingdom-minded. Every time you transfer wealth from the world and into your hands, you are taking dominion over that wealth and bringing it into the Kingdom of God. It is now in the possession of a Kingdom man or woman. It is now available to be used in the advancement of the Gospel over the earth. Every time you buy land, that piece of ground is now in Kingdom hands. Every time you make a business transaction, the wealth of the world has been transferred to the children of God. Deuteronomy 8:18 reminds us why we want this wealth: "that He may establish His covenant which He swore to your fathers, as it is this day." The wealth you generate is for a greater purpose than yourself. It is for the purpose of establishing God's covenant on the earth. There are billions of dollars worth of transactions taking place in the airwaves just above our heads. Why not reach up and take a few of these dollars from the hands of worldly men and put them in your hands, the hands of the righteous?

There should be something rising up in you even now that says, "Amen!" There should be a fire starting to burn in your heart that says, "I've been created for more. I'm better than this. I'm not going to bury my talent any longer. I want to take my place alongside the blessed and prosperous servants of God who are serving the Lord with their increase. I want to start today being prosperous and multiplying what I have been given. I want to finance the Gospel of the Kingdom of God throughout nations!"

If you say these things, you are pleasing to the Father. He rewards such people!

PROSPERITY IN THE EVERYDAY WORLD

What does prosperity look like? As individuals, it looks like we are growing closer to the Lord with every passing week. Sure, we go through trials and we go through troubles, but we stay glued to the Word of God. Every time we go through these times, we take another step higher and another step deeper. That's prosperity!

What does prosperity look like? In your marriage, it means that you fall deeper and deeper in love with your spouse. Your marriage is getting better with every passing anniversary. I have been married to Nicki since 1985 and I love her more now than ever. My love and adoration for her grows year-by-year. That's prosperity! What does prosperity look like? It looks like praying for people to be saved and they come to Christ. You have just multiplied yourself in the Kingdom of God. Another soul has been saved and another name written in the Lamb's Book of Life. That's prosperity!

What does prosperity look like? It looks like being able to get out of debt. Little by little, one bill at a time, you are able to mark "paid" on each one of them. People scratching off lottery tickets and checking the mailbox for millions hardly ever, if ever, experience this joy. You can get out of debt by making a little extra on a car payment every month, maybe by making a bi-monthly mortgage payment, putting a little extra each month on that debt until it's gone. Working your way out of debt, that's prosperity!

What does prosperity look like? It looks like working hard until you get promoted at work. You don't talk about your boss; you don't fight with everybody that you work with; you learn to get along with people; you learn how to shut your mouth and work hard and give an honest day's work and you don't let other people punch your time clock out. That's prosperity!

What does prosperity look like? It looks like accumulating wealth, one dollar at a time. It may be $100 now, then $1,000, then $10,000, then $100,000. It looks like a retirement fund and decent investments over a long term that creates dividends for the Kingdom of God and for your family. That's prosperity!

What does prosperity look like? It looks like your kids sitting around the dinner table in the evenings saying their prayers. It's when they look to heaven with innocent eyes at night kneeling beside their beds and you hear them pray for you. It looks like a church play or musical program when your child quotes scripture when it's time to say their lines. It's when the teenager says, "No," to peer pressure at school. That's prosperity!

What does prosperity look like? It looks like friends who love you and like to laugh when you laugh, cry when you cry, sing when you sing and share the load that you're carrying. It looks like those special people who will be there for the rest of your life. That's prosperity.

What does prosperity look like? It looks like your children when they get married and they are going to have their own children and that these grandchildren of yours are able to walk with God and enjoy victories that their grandparents fought and won for them. That's prosperity!

Prosperity is increase. It's the ability to keep moving forward when times are tough and the hindrances are many. It's the ability to create generational blessings that will increase throughout the years of your life and break those curses that have haunted your family. It means that you dare to dream a dream, set a goal too big to achieve in your lifetime and then spend the rest of your life trying. It means that you never say never and hate the word, quit. It means that you are going to move forward and take control over your life and not allow others to dictate your life to you any longer. It means that you're sick and tired of not being able to finance the dreams and visions of your church. You want to make sure that the man or woman of God, in whose vision you serve, is able to fulfill each one of their God-given dreams.

This is the kind of life that pleases God. This is what He wants for all of His kids. Are you ready to break the spirit of poverty?

LOOKING INTO THE POVERTY MIRROR

The spirit of poverty is like a mirror. When you look into it you see yourself as blurred and deformed from the way that God has made you. It is false reality through which your self-image is diffused. When you operate out of a spirit of poverty, it paints a fictitious picture over who you really are for the specific purpose of keeping you from Kingdom increase and multiplication. It will tell you that you are unwanted, ignorant, flawed, rejected and unable to live a blessed and joyful life.

Do you really believe that God is glorified with us seeing ourselves that way? Do you think that God is pleased with us suffering under the spirit of poverty? I think not. In fact, how would you feel if your kids felt this way? They always felt like a loser. They never felt loved by you or anyone else. They did not believe that they had the ability to succeed in life. They never tried anything new because they knew that they would fail. How would that make you feel? How do you think it makes God feel when we walk under a spirit of poverty? I can tell you – worse! He is trying to free you up right now from this insidious spirit that has controlled and convinced you that you will never prosper. This spirit has kept the church from moving forward for centuries.

> (1) The poverty mirror keeps us hidden under a canopy of despair.

We say things like, "I'll never amount to anything." It makes us say things like, "Nothing good ever happens to me." It's a mindset that says, "I never catch a break…I was born on the wrong side of the tracks…I'll never overcome my past." This poverty mirror keeps us in despair by reminding us of our past sins and our present circumstances. It brings up the past and says that you will never be spiritual because you had an abortion; because you have been divorced; because you cheated on your spouse; because you have been a thief.

> (2) The poverty mirror focuses on what we don't have instead of what we do have.

A person hears an idea and shoots it down immediately because they don't think they have the necessary resources available to make it happen. Someone makes a suggestion about how to succeed in business but the person looking into the poverty mirror dismisses it because they don't believe that it's possible. A pastor preaches about a new dream or vision that the Lord has given him or her but the congregation doesn't receive it because they don't believe that they have the money, the manpower or the means. It falls on deaf ears because of the poverty spirit has stolen the seed.

> (3) The poverty mirror makes us feel lesser than other people.

It will keep you from your destiny by making you believe lies about yourself. You feel so inferior to the five-talent people in the world. It makes you think the best that you can do is bury your talent and survive until Jesus returns. It keeps you believing that you will never win in life and that success is always beyond your grasp. It will persuade you that everyone else is smarter than you, better looking than you, more blessed than you, more spiritual than you and more loved than you. It will make you feel like you're coming to plate already two strikes down. In that mirror, you see yourself as lesser than other people, depleted emotionally and spiritually. You see yourself as barely hanging on most of the time.

I pastor people who feel that way their entire lives. Every Sunday when you ask, "How are you doing?" they answer, "Oh, I am hanging in there." When I hear people say that, I would like to say, "Then let go!" The fact is, we aren't hanging onto anything that belongs to God. He's hanging onto us! If we believe that it's our efforts and power that keeps us connected to God, then we are deceived! We are in the palm of His hand, not the other way around. Perhaps the problem is that we are hanging onto stuff that God wants us to let go of!

> (4) The poverty mirror makes us feel like an odd ball and an outcast.

From the moment they encounter a crowd, they have identified themselves as the outsider. Everyone else is prettier. Everyone else is smarter. Everyone else has it all together. Everyone else knows what to say. Everyone else knows each other. Everyone else knows where to go. Everyone else knows what to do. Everyone else is having a good time. People who gaze at themselves in the poverty mirror instantly identify themselves as strange, ugly and an outcast.

The Bible says in Proverbs 23:7, "as he thinks in his heart so is he." When you see yourself as an outcast, you make yourself act like one in the crowd. The moment you walk in the door, you are walking in the identity that you saw in the poverty mirror. You believe that about yourself and then act that way. Literally, you put off an aura that says to everyone in the room, "Don't mind me, I'm an odd ball." So everyone treats you that way.

You have the power to change the way people see you, not by losing 50 pounds and looking like a supermodel, but by breaking the spirit of poverty over your life. You have the ability to change the way people treat you by changing the way you treat yourself. You have the ability to change your environment. You have the ability to change your destiny. You have the ability to change the outcome. You have the ability to change the rest of your life. You have the ability to make many friends. You have the ability to be successful. You have been given every tool that you need as a child of God to have fruitfulness and prosperity. It starts by changing how you feel about yourself. Stop looking in the poverty mirror.

Both the Apostles Paul and James agree that there is another mirror available for Christians. When we view ourselves in this mirror we see who we are in Christ and are then changed into that image from glory to glory. It says in II Corinthians 3:18, "But we all, with unveiled face, beholding as in a mirror the glory of the Lord, are being transformed into the same image from glory to glory, just as by the Spirit of the Lord." Again, about this mirror, it says in James 1:23,

"For if anyone is a hearer of the word and not a doer, he is like a man observing his natural face in a mirror." The Bible is a mirror that reveals your true reflection, which you are in Christ. When we read the word and believe it, we are changed from an image of poverty to one of prosperity and increase!

That's why the Bible says that the old man was crucified with Christ. How much deader can you get than crucified? The Bible doesn't say your old man has been put on the shelf. The Bible doesn't say your old man has been given a ticket to another state for a vacation. It doesn't say that your old man has been put on ice for a little bit. It doesn't say that your old man has been put in the penalty box. It says your old man was put in the graveyard, dead and gone! Why do you keep digging up the old man and putting him back on yourself? You should dig up your talent and use it for God's glory but leave the skeleton behind!

The Bible says in II Corinthians 5:17 that we are "new creatures." This verse means that we are a brand new species of individuals. You and I represent humanity at its best. The Bible is so clear about our new identity that it says your old identity is killed and you have been resurrected in Christ as a new man. Isn't that awesome?

> (5) The poverty mirror gives us an intense fear of failure, rejection and the unknown.

These three specific areas are the most common: fear, rejection and the unknown. That's why people with the spirit of poverty never do great things for the Kingdom of God. They are afraid to do great things. They never step out in faith because they are afraid of failure. Faith necessitates risk. If it's not risky, it is not faith. These people have a fear of rejection, so they never step out and try to make new friends. The fear of the unknown is a fear that says, "I am not going to step in areas where I have never been before." That spirit of fear has infected the children of God and the church of Jesus Christ. That's the reason why entire congregations repeatedly say, "We have never done it that way before."

If you listen carefully you'll hear people in the church express the spirit of poverty all the time by saying things like, "We can't do that! Why are they dancing up there? What are those flags? We never had flags before. Why do you have to have flags? Why do you have to have those gowns? We have got gowns now. Drums! Why do we have drums? We never had drums before? A band? Why do you have to have a band? Grandpa and Grandma never needed a band to worship God!" And so we get stuck in a circle-the-wagon syndrome, burying our talents because we are suffering from a spirit of poverty that makes us fearful of the unknown. In fact, I want to tell you that Satan loves the spirit of poverty, not only because of what it does to society, but because of what it does to the church. Because so goes the church, so goes society.

(6) The poverty mirror convinces us that people owe us something.

They are on the welfare roles and make up the entitlement generation. When they look into the poverty mirror, they see a weakling who can't help himself or herself. "I'm so weak," they believe, "I'm so ignorant. I'm such a loser. I can't help myself. I have got to have the government help me." This sense of being too frail to help themselves is a result of the face of poverty that looks back at them from the mirror.

Pleasing God With Your Increase

(7) The poverty mirror makes us see ourselves as a victim.

These one talent people are always bemoaning the fact that someone has cheated them out of their talents. Somebody else is to blame. Someone has been mean to them and that's why they are failures. Someone short-changed them. Someone gave them the short end of the stick. From the moment they were born until now, life has been unfair and they have always been picked on and taken advantage of. That's why they cannot succeed.

(8) The poverty mirror makes us afraid of being too big, being too successful, and going too far.

You hear it all the time, "Well, let's not go too far. Let's not go too fast. Let's not get too big." What would happen if the church did go too far, too fast and got too big? It might start to look like the Book of Acts! This kind of mentality is like the people standing on the shore warning Christopher Columbus about going too far. We have this flat world syndrome in the church, don't we? We stand on the shoreline as some brave Christopher Columbus goes sailing off into the unknown with a vision from God. We voice our warnings, "Go ahead, we will never see you again. When you fall off the edge of the earth, don't come back crying to us!"

I have had people tell me that the church I pastor is just too big for them. What are you going to do when your grandson wants to get saved, turn him away because we have reached our limit? Who is the one that gets turned away? Is it your son or your daughter? How about your Grandma? You can stand at the door and say, "You can't come in here today and get saved. We're too big now. We've come too far!"

It's time to break the poverty mirror and start living out of our Biblical identity!

GOD IS PLEASED WITH SUCCESS

I have heard people say that when they started getting real successful, they started feeling guilty. I talked to a business owner one time about his place in the marketplace and in the kingdom. I was affirming this man and blessing him to sign bigger contracts and make more money. God is raising up business people like him and blessing them to go out and make millions for the church. They are looking to lay great wealth at the apostle's feet (see Acts 4:37). He told me at the end of our conversation, "This is the first time in my life that I don't feel guilty for making money." Did you get that? Guilty! This man was feeling guilty for doing what God rewarded those two servants for doing – creating wealth!

Do you know what's holding back the vision of many men and women of God? The number one thing that hinders the vision of the church is a lack of financial resource. We can't do it because we can't fund it. Men and women of God have great visions and dreams for outreach where people are blessed and entire cities and nations are touched by the gospel. But who is going to pay for it?

Most churches are having a hard time advancing the Kingdom of God because only about 10% of the people in the pews actually tithe. I believe that men and woman of God are going to dream dreams and see visions in the last days just like Joel 2:28 says, "And it shall come to pass afterward That I will pour out My Spirit on all flesh; Your sons and your daughters shall prophesy, Your old men shall dream dreams, Your young men shall see visions." This was the verse that Peter quoted on the Day of Pentecost that describes the work of the Holy Spirit within the church. God is anointing people who are prosperous in the world in order to create revenue streams for the purpose of funding these Spirit-filled dreamers and visionaries. Maybe you are one of them. But first, the spirit of poverty must be broken.

Why did my friend feel guilty for making money and being prospered? He felt guilty because he was told all his life that money was evil. He felt guilty for being blessed because many pastors who had preached to him suffered from a spirit of poverty. I grew up hearing about the evils of money even though the churches we attended didn't have enough to fund great visions. It was always referred to as, "Filthy lucre, filthy lucre!" That was, until the offering was being taken and then we heard how the church was on the verge of going broke and how God needed someone to give their lucre. After that, it was back to, "Filthy lucre, filthy lucre!"

Don't ever forget that one of the criteria for judgment is how we handle our money. God wants us to prosper so we can do something significant with our earnings. He is calling us out of the poverty mindset to allow the worldwide Kingdom invasion to begin.

CHAPTER 5

"Looking Through the Poverty Lens"

In the last chapter we looked at what people see when they view themselves in the poverty mirror and were held back by the poverty lid. In this chapter, we will discuss what people see when their view is turned towards God, other people and the world as they peer though the poverty lens.

SEEING GOD THROUGH THE POVERTY LENS

I want you to notice what the man said in verse 24 who had received one talent: "Lord, I knew that you were a hard man, reaping where you have not sown and gathering where you have not scattered, and I was afraid." He saw God as a hard man. And what kind of reaction did he have towards God? Fear. He was afraid of God in an unhealthy way. That fear paralyzed him and kept him from releasing the Lord's money for the purpose of increase.

The spirit of poverty will distort your vision of God as you see Him through the lens of poverty. You will see God as a hard man, a taskmaster. He will seem demanding, mean and impossible to please. You will have a tendency to believe that the only time that

God really moves is when he wants to pour out wrath. A hard man is one that has no compassion and no patience with imperfection. He is a kind of fly-off-the-handle-and-backhand-you-across-the-room kind of God. This is the way that many Christians see their Father in heaven because the spirit of poverty has robbed them of a clear view.

Do you know what I described? I described some of your fathers. And it's a natural thing to view God with a projected image of your earthly father. If you grew up with that kind of a hard man as a father, you are naturally going to see God the same way. And what is your reaction? Fear. And what does fear do? Fear makes you cower in the corner and hide your treasure. You don't want to take risks. You don't want to be bold. You don't want to go out and try new things because you're afraid. Just like many of us, the man that had the one talent had a distorted and perverse view of God. It's an unhealthy fear of God; that He was a hard man, somehow detached and uncaring, that moved this servant to hide his talent.

I want to tell you something that you need to settle in your mind right here and right now. God poured out his wrath on his Son and if you accept Jesus as a Savior, then you are a son or daughter of grace and mercy. God's entire wrath was poured out on Jesus and He has fully paid your sin-debt and mine. Now, God expresses only love and grace towards His children. Are we perfect? No. But God loves us anyway, kind of like you and I do with our children. Though they need corrected from time to time and don't always obey like they should, we do not disown them and turn them away.

The spirit of poverty works alongside the spirit of religion to steal this precious truth from the church. We strive to earn the favor of God that we already possess in Jesus. We work and work to measure up to a standard that Jesus already achieved for us. All that's left for us to do in the process of salvation is to believe. Faith will destroy the spirit of religion AND the spirit of poverty. Faith will give us peace within our hearts because no matter what, we know that we have peace with God. Faith will give us rest in the storms of life because we know that God loves us and nothing can separate us from that love!

SEEING OTHERS THROUGH THE POVERTY LENS

The spirit of poverty will also affect the way that you see other people. What will happen is that the spirit of poverty will make you jealous of what other people possess. We need to learn to rejoice when other people are blessed and thank God for their increase. Then we need to draw close to that person in order to learn the secrets of their success. God will set up these situations to see if we are going to humble ourselves and learn from a blessed person or be jealous of them and criticize their prosperity. It happens when you really wanted that job and someone else got it. You really wanted that car but someone else is driving it. You really wanted that boyfriend but someone else is dating him. You really wanted that position but someone else is attaining it. While we should be rejoicing when other people are blessed, a spirit of poverty jumps up and starts doing the math, "They have five talents and I only have one. That's not fair!"

Until you learn to rejoice in another person's blessings, you will never be free from a spirit of poverty. You will never quite be trustworthy to receive God's best blessings. A spirit of poverty will keep you from receiving from others because you will feel threatened and suspicious of people who walk in a greater financial blessing than you do. You will avoid them and keep yourself isolated from receiving those same blessings. People influenced by the spirit of poverty will be distrustful of the very people from whom they need to be learning. It will keep them circling in the same field of lack year after year and generation after generation.

A person suffering from a spirit of poverty will see someone who has what he or she wants and will make a comment like, "Who do they think they are? They just think they're better than everyone else." Apprehension and misgiving fill their mind with critical thoughts and they become appalled by these blessed people. The spirit of poverty has made them feel lesser than those people all their life and when they see someone who has been successful and prosperous, they are particularly sensitive and insecure to their own perceived inferiority. They instantly assume the worst about the individual and create an escape from having to admit their own failure and learning the other person's secrets of success by saying, "Oh, she thinks she's so hot with her new car and nice clothes. Praise God, I don't need all of that to be happy." It never occurs to them to learn from that successful person. Instead, they criticize them. A spirit of poverty keeps us away from the very thing that we need in order to be blessed and advance the Kingdom of God.

It has been my experience that people of affluence are sometimes recipients of greater prejudice in the church than people of poverty. When a poor person walks into the room people often feel natural sympathy and sorrow for them but when a wealthy person walks into the same room, everyone begins to judge them by their car, clothes and jewelry. Almost instantly, if someone has any pizzazz, if someone has any style, if someone is educated or if they are from the big city, they are viewed with suspicion and dislike by those who are influenced by a poverty mindset. Has anyone ever stopped to think that perhaps God has sent people like this to the church for the purpose of creating wealth for the Kingdom of God and helping the poor person? We need to thank God for both and minister to each one equally.

It is a spirit of poverty that is erecting a wall to keep you from receiving an anointing that God has for you. It's an anointing to do what the first two servants did in Matthew 25. It's an anointing to live out in obedience the first command of the Kingdom of God to subdue the earth and take dominion. It's an anointing to answer the Lord's Prayer when He prayed for God's will to be done on earth as it is in heaven.

The spirit of poverty will keep your church from receiving new impartations from people who have something you don't. When someone says, "Oh, they think they've got something we don't," they might be right! God will send key people at key times to impart and release a new anointing in the lives of individuals and congregations, alike. The poverty spirit will short-circuit this even before it ever takes place by swelling up with disdain and distrust concerning those who walk in a greater blessing. Even though we may be crying out to God for more, when He sends it, we usually miss it. In that scenario, Satan has cut us off from receiving anything new and we are left forever to walk in those things that we already have.

I had a vision once about the area of the country in which I live. It was surrounded with a wall that looked like the old Berlin Wall. We were standing there just looking at this wall collectively wishing that we could cross over to the other side. We knew that there were good things on the other side and if we could just make it over, we would be blessed. Every now and again there would be someone rise up from our midst and climb up on someone's shoulders. This person would reach up to the top of the wall. Everybody else standing around would say, "Who does he think he is? He just walks all over people. Look at him, he's promoting himself on the shoulders of those poor people." With that, they would begin to throw stones and bottles at this person until they would fall off the shoulders of the people. Everyone would applaud and say, "There you go. Now you're on our level again." And then like zombies, we would all turn and stare at the wall again, wishing we could get over it.

A little bit later someone else would rise up. Here would come the bottles and rocks again to bring him back down. "He is just getting the big head," I heard people say. "He just thinks he's better than anyone else. We had to bring him down a notch, praise God." Then everyone returned to the wall.

What didn't occur to the people in my vision was that God was trying to raise people up on the shoulders of the church so that they could reach the top of the wall. After getting on top, they would reach down and begin to pull others up and over. Standing on people's shoulders was a necessary way of reaching the top. It represented men and women of God who are visionaries. They hold the keys to freedom for the rest of the church and society. The spirit of poverty gets involved and jealousy is aroused against those people who get promoted because it makes others feel inferior and insecure. So instead of helping promote those key people who can climb to new heights and help us achieve the same, we take aim with our stones of criticism and bottles of rebellion because we want to "put them in their place."

Some of you reading this book are dreamers and visionaries. I want to encourage you to keep reaching new heights in spite of the stones and bottles that are flying your way. Some of you are marketplace people. I want to encourage you to put these dreamers on your shoulders and work to finance their dreams and visions. Others of you are stone throwers and bottle hurlers. I want to encourage you to put down your projectiles and shout out as much praise and encouraging words as you can, knowing that when others reach a new level, it won't be long until you reach that same place.

God uses people in His Kingdom. God uses leaders and he anoints people to help the entire Body of Christ. These men and women are key holders. God will strategically bring people to you during specific seasons in your life that will hold keys to your success. You have got to let them unlock the doors that you cannot unlock for yourself. They have keys for you and you have a key that someone else needs. That's how the kingdom works. That's why we need each other. The spirit of poverty, however, will keep you perpetually mired in poverty because you look at others with suspicion, criticism, and jealousy - people who have come with more than you in order to help you reach your destiny. How you treat them will determine your future. This is another way that the spirit of poverty keeps us in disunity and detachment from one another. Let's change that!

SEEING LIFE THROUGH THE POVERTY LENS

A spirit of poverty affects the way that you see life. It affects the way that you see the universe around you. When you view your life and future destiny through a lens of poverty, you will become convinced that things will never get any better. It is never going to change. The spirit of poverty will say that the best you can do is just barely hang on because you will never win any significant victories. The best you can do is to just survive until Jesus comes back. The spirit of poverty is supported nearly every week in churches by the testimonies of the people and the theology from the pulpit. You will hear things like, "Well, you all pray for me that I will just hold on until Jesus comes back." Then another well-meaning saint will affirm, "Life is so tough and the world so sinful. You all pray for me because I'm barely hanging on. Just pray that I will make it until Jesus comes back." I remember being about sixteen years old and hearing saints of God give testimonies like these and I would think to myself, "Dear God, if they have been doing this for 50 years and can do no better than that, I might as well give up now!"

I remember seeing a movie at the youth camp where people got their heads cut off in a guillotine for not getting a 666 tattoo on their foreheads. The Antichrist was killing everyone and the church was going down like the Titanic. I thought to myself, "Oh God, is this what I've got to look forward to?" The picture I received of the last day's church was one where people were running around defeated and hiding in caves and cellars. There was no power, no anointing and no victory. In fact, most people were giving in and going to the tattoo parlor. I was really depressed and discouraged over it and walked away from fellowship with God for a season in my life. I remember telling my aunt, "Your lucky because you're old." She said, "What?" I said, "You know, you are going to be with Jesus before the church has a great falling away and everyone gets their heads chopped off."

That's all I ever heard about the future of the church. The preachers would talk about the great falling away and how nobody wants to be saved and serve Jesus anymore. They would point to the fact that their churches were dead and empty as proof that the great falling away was underway and we were living in the last days. The guillotines were just around the corner and tattoo parlors were popping up everywhere. I was reminded constantly that hard times were on the way, the Antichrist is going to be victorious and the world was doomed. How much faith did that stir up? How much optimism? How much hope? How much passion? That really makes me want to get saved and carry on with Jesus, how about you?

The only hope they gave people in those days was that Jesus is coming back and everyone will escape the conflict like the British troops at Dunkirk. We looked forward to the rapture like a call of retreat to battered and defeated troops. There was no call to conquer the world. We were like prisoners waiting for our day of release from the world. We sang about being released. We dreamed about being released. We preached and testified about being released. The problem was that in the mean-time, we were doing precious little in the way of Kingdom advancement. After all, why advance the Kingdom around the earth if the Antichrist is just going to take it back? Why build up the church if they are all just going to fall away? The best message we had to offer was the hope that we can hunker down and endure this old evil world until the call to retreat sounds.

This is an escapism mentality that is borne out of a spirit of poverty. It says that we will never have victory. The only thing that we have to look forward to is defeat after defeat. If the devil gets you to believe in that, then your life will follow your expectations and you will be defeated. Your life will reflect your faith and you will live in a prison awaiting the great escape that will come some day. You will live in the expectation of defeat for the rest of your life.

But you can break that spirit of poverty!

SEVEN WAYS TO BREAK THE SPIRIT OF POVERTY

I will conclude this chapter with seven ways to break that spirit of poverty in your life. Although there may be many more steps in the process, these seven will get you started.

(1) You must believe that God is good and loves you.

It all starts with God. Every great revelation in your life will start with a new revelation of God. The first thing to break the spirit of poverty is to attack its guardian, the spirit of religion. This happens when we choose to believe that God is a good God who loves us and wants to bless us. He wants to prosper us. He wants to heal us. He wants our kids to be blessed and protected. He wants to be with us and know us all intimately. He will never leave us nor forsake us. He wants to talk to us. He wants to answer our prayers. Until you come to peace with these truths, you will forever struggle with a spirit of poverty.

> (2) <u>You must see yourself as righteous</u> and <u>worthy to be blessed by the Blood of Jesus Christ.</u> *Prov 23:7*

If you are still trying to prove your worth to God, you will never do it. If you are still trying to earn God's favor by your works, you'll be frustrated. If you're trying to perform so that God will love you, you will always feel like a failure. You have got to know that Jesus finished the work and your faith in him has made you righteous. Period. The spirit of poverty will start to be broken in your life when you get a vision that you are the righteousness of Jesus Christ before God.

> (3) <u>You must expect that good things are going to happen to you in every situation</u>.

Every time something bad happens, start looking for the blessing. David said in Psalm 23:5, "You prepare a table before me in the presence of my enemies." When your enemies surround you, start looking for the table! God orders your steps. He knows when bad things are coming. Although life presents us with tough situations that might cause a temporary setback, God saw it coming and has planned a way to bless you through it all. In order to escape the grasp of the spirit of poverty, you have to be able to battle in faith and war with hope that goes beyond apparent circumstances. You have got to walk in the expectation that good things are going to happen to you.

> (4) You need to applaud other people's success.

As I said earlier, you need to understand that when other people succeed, it will help you, too. Don't be afraid to share the podium. When you get enough people on your podium, God will show you a higher level. When you help everybody up on that level, God will show you that there is even a higher step for you to climb. Your climbing will come to a stop, however, if you ever get to the point where you feel threatened by other people's success. I need you to be successful and you need me to be successful. When I succeed, you succeed. When you succeed, I succeed. We're connected together in this entity called the Body of Christ and that's a beautiful thing.

> (5) You have to see the transfer of wealth as a Godly principle.

Until you see that wealth is a Kingdom issue, you will always struggle with how money connects with the gospel of Jesus Christ. Often this disconnect is maintained by a spirit of mammon or what is simply called, "the love of money." The prophet saw that the wealth of the Gentiles would be brought to God's covenant people. Solomon saw the wealth of the wicked laid up for the righteous.

In order to break the spirit of poverty, you need to understand the message of the transfer of wealth that's happening in the world today and have a desire to participate in it. That simply means that there is wealth and riches in the world today that is in the possession of ungodly hands and the children of God are allowed to pray and to work hard with divine strategies in order to see that wealth brought into the church for the establishment of the Kingdom of God. God has made a plan to get that wealth into your hands as the righteous seed of God so that it can be released for the work of the Kingdom of God.

(6) <u>You must understand that everything that you have belongs to God</u>.

If you do not understand that everything you have belongs to God, then you are a danger to yourself and to everyone else around you! If you want to be rich only to serve your own self-indulgence, then the principles in this book are not for you! You've missed it! You have to be totally and completely committed to God's Kingdom and your local church in order to see your life move into true prosperity. Jesus said in Matthew 6:21, "For where your treasure is, there your heart will be also." If you want to find a man's heart, look for his treasure. If you are not sowing your treasure into your local church and into other Kingdom-minded ministries where you are at today, then don't expect to be blessed with anything more than what you already have. You must show your heart for the things of the Kingdom of God by placing your treasure in the right places immediately.

What that will do for you is help free you up from the burden of keeping what you have and from the fear of losing it. When the burden of creating wealth gets heavy, you can remind yourself that it was never yours to begin with. When you fear the reprisals and ruined reputations that financial hard times can bring, remember that none of it was yours in the first place. It really frees you up.

(7) <u>You have to give, let go, release and sow</u>.

Do you know how to prove that all your treasure belongs to

God? By giving him the first 10%. You are not honest until you give 10% and you are not generous until you give 11%. God has told us that if we would give Him the first 10% (tithe), then He would bless the other 90%. You have got to give, let go, release, and sow. Give it! Release it! Let go! Get it out of your hands! Sow your seed and be a generous person where you are at today and then you can expect God to give you more.

The journey of freedom has begun!

CHAPTER 6

"Your Promise Needs a Blessing"

Breaking the spirit of poverty starts with being able to release, being able to give. The man that received the five talents traded those talents. And what do you do when you trade? You have to release what you have in order to get something back. The man with two talents also released what he had been given. But the man with one talent held onto it. He was afraid to release what was in his hand. I'm sure the man with one talent probably thought, "Well, I don't have enough to give. I'm not rich like those other guys. I'm poor. This is all I've got. If I release it, I will have nothing."

As we have talked about breaking the spirit of poverty, one of the things that I've tried to do is give you all sorts of ideas about how to prosper. I have talked about being mentored, investing in yourself, getting an education, working hard, being dedicated, being patient, etc. While all of these are Biblical steps in breaking the spirit of poverty and walking in prosperity, still, the first step in breaking the spirit of poverty is learning how to release what's in your hand. Until you and I learn how to be cheerful givers to the Lord's work, we will never move into Biblical prosperity.

I don't want to be labeled as the type of minister that says all you have to do in order to walk in prosperity is give me your money! I don't want you to hear that. But we cannot ignore what the Bible says about giving an offering, "But this I say: He who sows sparingly will also reap sparingly, and he who sows bountifully will also reap bountifully (II Corinthians 9:6)." The next verse says, "So let each one give as he purposes in his heart, not grudgingly or of necessity; for God loves a cheerful giver." We cannot allow this truth to be lost because somebody takes it to an extreme. History verifies the testimony of Gamaliel in Acts 5:36-37 concerning the large number of counterfeit messiahs who emerged during the time of the incarnation of Christ. Why did this happen? Because whenever God is ready to do something genuine, Satan tries to discredit the genuine by introducing a flood of counterfeits. But the fact that there is a counterfeit is a testimony to the existence of a genuine!

If you have ever heard a counterfeit message on prosperity, then you can rest assured that there is a genuine message somewhere. We need a balanced message of prosperity in the church that teaches the blessedness of giving, discipline in spending, wisdom in investing, diligence in working, patience in saving and the purity of ambition. This, along with faith, will work together to break the spirit of poverty and replace it with a Kingdom message of dominion and increase that will lead to the advancement of the Kingdom of God around the earth.

IS THE SEED IN YOUR HAND OR IN THE GROUND?

Learning to release what you have is the first step in breaking the spirit of poverty. If you have a seed in your pocket, you have a promise. But that's all you have. That promise does not become a blessing until you mix it with faith and release your seed. Only then will you have the possibility of increase and fruitfulness. A spirit of poverty has a pocket full of seeds but is afraid to plant them because it fears the idea of losing them. That's why someone who walks under a spirit of poverty dreams about a great harvest but never experiences it. Slowly, they eat up all of their seed instead of planting it. The end condition of the person is worse than the beginning. This is why Jesus said of the man with one talent after he lost it, "Therefore take the talent from him, and give it to him who has ten talents. For to everyone who has, more will be given, and he will have abundance; but from him who does not have, even what he has will be taken away (Matthew 25:28-29)."

Eventually, the person who is afraid to release their wealth will lose it completely. Slowly, the unplanted seeds in their pocket will disappear while everyone else's seeds will multiply in the ground, bringing about a great and mighty harvest.

Seeds do not multiply and bear fruit until they are released into the ground. Jesus said that He, Himself, was a seed and that He had to be put into the ground and die (John 12:23-24). He had to be released from this life in order to be a resurrection seed that would multiply and increase into much fruit. You and I are results of that seed! We are the results of Jesus releasing His life in faith and being put into the ground.

ABRAHAM'S PROMISE NEEDED A BLESSING

You can have a promise without a blessing. That promise is the seed in your pocket. It will become a blessing when it is released. The seed will multiply and produce fruit when it is released and planted. The spirit of poverty doesn't care how many seeds you have in your possession. Those promises and prophecies are common. There are multitudes of believers walking around with a pocket full of seeds. If you believe in prophetic things, you are probably walking around with all of these prophecies like little seeds in your pocket. We hear that God is going to do this or God is going to do that. We have promises of healing, prosperity, salvation, deliverance, freedom, great growth, etc. We have a promise but not a blessing.

Hebrews 7:6 says, "but he (Melchizedek)...received tithes from Abraham and blessed him who had the promises." Abraham had a promise without a blessing. He had seeds without any fruit. Although God had promised him a son, that seed had not become a reality. The father of the Jews needed a blessing upon his promise. This is where Melchizedek comes into the picture. He was a king of Salem and a priest of the Most High God. Every priest called by God has the ability to bless people. The priests of the Old Testament were commanded by God to bless the people of Israel (Numbers 3:22-27). When Jesus sent out His 12 disciples and later another 70 servants, He told them to bless the homes in which they stayed (Luke 10:5-6). The people who provided for their physical needs were to be blessed with a spiritual blessing. Paul understood this concept when he said, "If we have sown spiritual things for you, is it a great thing if we reap your material things (I Corinthians 9:11)." God was setting up Abraham to receive a blessing upon his promise. But first, Abraham had to plant his seed!

Abraham had defeated four kings as described in Genesis 14. Everybody knows that kings have great wealth. So when Abraham defeated not one, not two, not three, but four kings, Abraham received the wealth of four kingdoms. Abraham was already a wealthy man at this point. The Bible says as much in Genesis 13:2. He also had a standing army of 318 men who were born among his servants (Genesis 14:14). Can you imagine how much wealth Abraham had to create in order to maintain a standing army of that size?

After attacking and defeating the armies of these four kings, Melchizedek met Abraham on his journey. He had the wealth of those four kings in his possession. When Abraham met Melchizedek, he released his wealth to the king/priest of Salem. He gave him ten percent of his spoils from those four kingdoms. In return, Melchizedek blessed Abraham and his promise. The seed that Abraham gave was not as much a blessing for Melchizedek as it was to Abraham.

What I want you to see is that Abraham had promises, but those promises did not become blessings until AFTER he had sowed financially into Melchizedek's life. The moment that Abraham released his wealth to the king/priest, he received a blessing upon his promise. Again, that's what the Hebrew writer said in Hebrews 7:6, "but he (Melchizedek)...received tithes from Abraham and blessed him who had the promises." From that moment on, the promises of God began to become reality in Abraham and Sarah's life. In the following chapter, God makes a blood covenant with them. Not long after that, Abraham received his promised son, Isaac. Indeed, Abraham's promise was blessed when he released his seed.

GOD IS LOOKING FOR PEOPLE WHO WILL RELEASE THEIR SEED

There is no doubt in my mind that God is raising up people like Abraham who are going to help finance the Kingdom of God. These people need to be Kingdom-minded people. They need to understand that being successful is not enough. They are moving into a state of being significant. Success is measured by how much you have. Significance is measured by how much you give. God will bless people who want to stand behind His worldwide Kingdom advancement. He will release manifold blessings upon them and give them the power to create wealth, transferring it from the hands of the world and into the hands of men and women of God around the world who have given their lives to preach the message of salvation to humanity. Are you one of them?

People with the spirit of poverty, however, will never walk in significance. They will never receive these blessings like Abraham did because they are afraid to release their talent. They would rather bury it. Therefore, in the end, they even lose what little bit they have. What a shame!

God wants to bless you. He wants you to walk in multiplication and increase. He wants to bless your promise; bring fruit from your seed. But first, you have to sow it! You have to release what you have in order to receive more. Breaking the spirit of poverty starts with sowing the seed that you have. You may not have the ransom of four kings, but you do have something in your hand. Don't compare yourself with the five talent people and the two talent people. What is in your hand? Whatever it is, start there. And the principle is that when you release that seed and you sow financially, then you have a right to draw blessings from wherever you sow your seed. You have a right to eat the fruit of the field into which you have made an investment. You have a right to receive a blessing on your promise just like Abraham did!

FINDING GOOD SOIL FOR YOUR SEED

Let's make something clear: Melchizedek didn't need Abraham's money. How do I know this? Because Melchizedek was a king. He didn't meet Abraham on the way back from the battle and say, "Abraham, I'm telling you Jerusalem's electric bill can't hardly be paid and we are going to have to turn the lights out unless we get some help." Therefore, Abraham's giving was not out of sympathy but was given in faith. Abraham was also smart enough to recognize good soil when he saw it. He recognized the anointing on that king because he was also a priest of the Most High. Abraham had a generous heart and wanted to support God's man. In return, he was blessed with this great man's anointing. Abraham saw that his seed was able to create an exchange with the man of God and both would receive increase. I can see God in heaven applauding both of them. Neither had the spirit of poverty. They both traded and received more, advancing the Kingdom of God in both camps.

There is a mentality in the church sometimes that says, "I need to sow my seed where it is needed." I hear people say, "C'mon honey, let's leave this church. They're doing well without us. They don't need our money. Let's go find someone who has nothing and we'll sow our seed there." I want to suggest to you that there is a reason why some soil produces life and other soil does not. If you were a farmer, would you find a field that is already growing something or would you find a lifeless desert in which to sow your seed?

There are a lot of people who think that way. They may be giving alms every Sunday but they are not planting a seed and multiplying their blessing. Unlike Abraham, they walk right past the Melchizedeks in their life and look for people who have less than them. Instead of sowing a seed in good soil that has a chance to multiply and increase, they waste their seed in ground that has little possibility of bearing fruit. Alms are given to those in need, but a seed is given to those from whom we can receive a blessing from God. We will discuss this in more detail in a later chapter.

FIVE-TALENT PEOPLE

Are you a one-talent person? I wonder how many of us identify with the one-talent guy? How many people when they read this story immediately identify with the one-talent guy? Do you feel like you are living in his shoes? It's amazing to me that the one-talent man was only 33% of the Master's servants and yet 90% of the Body of Christ identifies with him. Ask how many people in any given congregation feel like the guy with one talent and the great majority of people will raise their hand. Why doesn't anybody identify with the five-talent guy? I'll tell you why: Because we all feel like a bunch of losers. The spirit of poverty has blinded us to four of our five talents.

God wants to change the mentalities of the church. We have been running around like a bunch of misfits and screwballs holding onto that identity like a bunch of nobodies. "We're just a poor bunch of workin' people," we'll say in a humble voice. "We ain't got much, never had much and never will have very much." We confess our faith in poverty, believing that all the Lord has for us is to barely get by. "All I need is just enough for my family, and me" we'll say in humble conclusion. Meanwhile, nobody can help the poor because we all see ourselves as the ones who are poor and in need of help. After all, we're not five-talent people, are we?

I know what the devil will tell you. He will team up with that spirit of poverty and fear to tell you that if you release what you have, then you will not have enough to survive. You will be in lack. He says this when he knows the opposite is true. We have already seen what Jesus said, "For to everyone who has, more will be given, and he will have abundance; but from him who does not have, even what he has will be taken away (Matthew 25:29)." Who will you believe?

You need to begin identifying with the five-talent person. Go look in the mirror and say to yourself, "I am a five-talent person!" Then you can quote Ephesians 1:3, "Blessed be the God and Father of our Lord Jesus Christ, who has blessed us with every spiritual blessing in the heavenly places in Christ." Did you get that? The Bible says that you have been blessed with EVERY spiritual blessing. I guess that makes you and me five-talent people, right? Instead of looking around at five-talent people with inferiority and jealousy, let's join them. Instead of dropping your chin and feeling sorry for yourself, see yourself as a blessed child of God. Instead of wasting your time hoping that a five-talent person might give you a little, why not release a few of your seeds to them and expect a return? Maybe the reason why you haven't seen those promises become blessings and those prophecies become reality is because you still have something in your hand that God is saying to release.

I'm ready to begin believing and acting like a five talent man. I'm ready for the exchange that will increase my talents to ten. How about you?

CHAPTER 7
"Learning to Release"

There is a drought in Israel. God's prophet, Elijah, had been taken care of miraculously by the ravens that fed him. But one day the birds stopped bringing their daily portions and the brook had dried up. It was then that God sent Elijah to a woman who was about to receive the greatest blessing of her life.

If it was going to be a miraculous day, it certainly did not look like it. While the prophet was making his way to her village, the widow was searching for sticks to use for her final meal. It was inevitable. Death was in the village. She planned to cook her final meal and then settle down like the rest of the village, waiting for death to come knocking at her door.

As she was gathering her sticks, the prophet came near. He looked different than most. This was probably due to the fact that he had been eating pretty well. While everyone else was emaciated and wasting away, Elijah was looking rather healthy and plump. He wandered into town and approached the widow woman as she was scouring about the landscape picking up sticks for the fire.

Elijah says to her, "What are you doing?" She replied, "I am gathering sticks because I have enough food for one meal, and I'm going to cook this meal for me and my son and then we will die like everyone else." At this point Elijah says something to her that I don't know if I would have been bold enough to say. He looked at this poor widow woman gathering sticks for her last meal and said, "Give to me first."

See, I don't know about you, but I would feel a lot more comfortable being the widow in that situation than Elijah. Can you imagine what the newspapers would say when they got ahold of that story? I can see it now, the local TV station does an expose' on the "The Plump Preacher Who Took the Widow's Last Meal." Who would want that type of publicity? Most of us would have much rather been the victim of such a scandal rather than the perpetrator. That's why we can say that it was a greater risk for Elijah to ask for an offering than it was for that lady to give it. It took just as much faith for Elijah to receive the seed as it did for the lady to sow it.

The reason that this story is important is because the spirit of poverty was about to be broken over that village and over that household. Elijah knew what he was doing. He didn't need what that woman had nearly as much as she needed what Elijah had. The miracle was on its way because good soil had just walked into town!

Now, no one would have blamed the poor widow for saying, "This is all I've got and I am not going to give you the last little bit of it. I am not going to sow this into your life. If I give you this, I will have none." This is how the spirit of poverty works. It looks at what a person doesn't have instead of what a person does have. It would have buried that meal by eating it and stealing from this lady the possibility of increase. In the end, in trying to keep it, she would have lost it all.

Instead of operating out of a poverty spirit, instead of eating her meal and being angry at the prophet for asking for it, she said, "Come on, sir." She fixed what little bit that she had left, put it on a plate and gave it to the preacher. She and her son watched with growling stomachs as the prophet gulped down every bite. She may have been living in a famine but she was not suffering from a spirit of poverty! Elijah took her last meal. She sowed her seed. She released her final meal to bless the man of God. In exchange, Elijah the prophet declared in verse 17, "For thus says the LORD God of Israel: 'The bin of flour shall not be used up, nor shall the jar of oil run dry, until the day the LORD sends rain on the earth.'"

There was miracle power that was unlocked in Elijah for that widow woman that he didn't even have for himself. He didn't have that miracle power for himself back at the brook Cherith. It dried up and he didn't have the ability to make more water. The miracle power that was in him didn't even come out for himself until a widow woman in faith sowed into him. She released her seed into him, the spirit of poverty was broken and the oil began to flow for her house and for the neighbors. Food was abundant.

There was abundance. There was increase. There was prosperity. There was multiplication. This is to be expected from a God who said in Philippians 4:19, "And my God shall supply all your need according to His riches in glory by Christ Jesus." What has God ever done that has not been extravagant? Although far from a five-talent woman in most people's opinion, when she released her seed, she unlocked a continuous flow of flour and oil from God's heavenly resources where there is no limit.

PRAISE GOD FOR THE OFFERING

We have to change our mentality towards offerings. Instead

of apologizing for taking offerings, pastors ought to rejoice for the opportunity. Instead of getting angry, the congregation ought to feel a sense of thankfulness. When Elijah comes to town offering good soil for our seed, we ought to act immediately and with great generosity. We should see such men and women of God, starting with our local pastors, as doing us a favor by allowing us to sow seed into their vineyard.

The spirit of poverty will make you feel like you are doing the church a favor when you give your finances. It does so because this insidious spirit wants you to focus on what you give instead of what you keep. If you really understood what was going on when you released those seeds, the spirit of poverty would be broken over your life like it was for the widow's family and you, too, could claim the right to begin to draw out a supernatural resource for your family.

Now, before somebody puts two and two together and gets five, let me go ahead and do it for you. A person might say, "Oh, Pastor Mark, it sounds like you're saying that you're buying your blessing. The more money you give, the more you get." No. It doesn't have anything to do with your money. It has to do with your faith. It is not your money that God rewards; it is your faith. The Bible says in Hebrews 11:6, "But without faith it is impossible to please Him, for he who comes to God must believe that He is, and that He is a rewarder of those who diligently seek Him." Just believing in God is not enough. We are also told that we must have faith in Him as a rewarder. How many people have faith that God exists and how many people have faith that God rewards? I would say that millions fit into the first category but very few ever walk far enough to live in the second part of that verse. There are very few things that Americans do that takes faith other than giving in the offering. There are very few things that many of the people reading this book will ever do more frequently and in greater quantity than stepping into the faith realm when it comes to sowing our financial seeds into worthwhile ministries. Doing this with an expectation of reward will please the Lord.

Someone might say, "Well, I am not interested in that prosperity message." Oh, you are not interested in it? Then why do you look in your box at work for your paycheck every two weeks? You are not interested in prosperity? Okay, next time you get a raise at work, deny it. When they want to pay you more money say, "No, no, you keep it. I don't believe in prosperity." The fact is, every time you cash your paycheck and accept a raise, you are making a testimony that you not only believe in prosperity, but you are working hard to obtain it.

I can hear some people saying now, "Well, God is not interested in my money." Oh, no? Then why in Matthew 25 when he talks about judgment did he talk about this parable of people that made money, created wealth, transferred wealth from the hands of the world into the hands of kingdom children? Why did God even use the parable if he wasn't interested in money? If God didn't care about money, then why did he say that the streets of Heaven were paved with gold? Why did he say the walls are made out of jasper and the gates of pearl? Do you know what they use jasper and pearls and gold for? Currency. It is ancient money. If Jesus was alive today and gave us those parables, he would say the streets are paved with dollar bills.

What does it say about God, that he used money and riches and gold to motivate us to live a holy life so we can go to Heaven? The same people who complain about the message of prosperity and live in a self-imposed spirit of poverty will stand up and testify about the mansion that God is preparing for them in Glory. Why do we talk about mansions if we don't believe in them?

I think it's time for a joke, don't you? This woman goes to Heaven and St. Peter meets her at the gate and says, "Follow me, I am going to show you your mansion." So they walk down golden streets. They walk by one mansion and she says, "Is that my mansion?"

He says, "No, no, no, it's on down here."

They walk by this other huge mansion. "Wow, is that my mansion?"

"No, that is not your mansion."

So they walk by another, and she's like, "Is that mine?"

"No."

"Is that mine?"

"No."

"Is that mine?"

"No."

So finally they walk down to the end of street, and there is this little shack about 12 feet by 12 feet. Peter says, "This is your mansion."

She says, "What is this? This is no mansion. How come mine doesn't look like the rest of these?"

Peter says, "Because we can only build with the material that you send up here!"

Again, why did God give us a parable about making money and how it would please God if creating wealth were not a part of His plan? Why would he create mansions and gold streets and talk about heaven with all of this fanfare and extravagance of materials if these things were disgusting to Him?

BACK TO EDEN...AGAIN

It is my opinion that the reason for such an allurement

attached to heaven goes back to the first kingdom mandate given to Adam and Eve. We are hardwired as human beings to take dominion and subdue the earth just like God said to our fore parents. It is in us. Every person reading this book, by the mere fact that you were a created human being, have an inward desire to take dominion and subdue the earth. That means conquer and dominate. That's why we mow our lawns, pull weeds, plant gardens, trim shrubs, clean our houses, build new buildings, wash our cars, sign bigger contracts, make more money, have more children, get more education, collect more ball cards, etc. It's all a part of subduing and dominating something.

If you own your own business, you want to be bigger. You want to hire more people, you want to make more money, you want to buy more trucks and sign more contracts. You don't have to feel guilty for that if you understand that it has a greater purpose than selfishness. It is for the advancement of the Kingdom of God.

You might say, "Pastor Mark, that doesn't sound right to me. To dominate and subdue sounds so militaristic and despotic, like a megalomaniac or something. Kind of like Hitler trying to take over the world." First, we are told as Kingdom people to, indeed, take over the world. In fact, Jesus said that the gospel of the kingdom would be preached around the world before He returns.

Secondly, the Kingdom of God is violent according to Jesus in Matthew 11:12. We cannot forget the militaristic aspects of the church. We are to be wearing armor, taking up arms and storming the gates of Hell.

Finally, don't forget what Satan likes to do. He does not have the power of creation so he can only use what already exists. He takes what God has created and makes it sinful by luring us to make it selfish. When the desire to dominate and subdue become selfish, then it becomes sin. God has given us all kinds of desires that are good and holy when they are submitted to God. But when they become selfish and self-centered, they become sinful. The same desire could be holy or sinful, depending on whether it is self-centered or God-centered; depending on whether it only benefits us or benefits others. That's why God punished the man who buried his talent. He was selfish. His desire to control and dominate was not outward focused but inward focused and this led him to selfishly hang onto what he should have released.

When we take what God created and we make it selfless and we submit to Him, then it becomes a holy thing. That's why the two servants who multiplied and prospered pleased God. They obeyed the Kingdom commands of God and gave it all back to Him. If your wealth is submitted to God and it is for a kingdom purpose, then it is a great thing and God will bless it abundantly. If you are suffering from a spirit of poverty and your wealth is buried in your back yard benefiting no one but yourself, then you are living under a curse.

ELISHA GETS HIS BLESSING

The second story of Elijah's ability to multiply seed is the episode of him and Elisha, his protégé and replacement. In the end, Elisha received a double portion of Elijah's anointing. This double portion represented the inheritance of the firstborn child. The journey started when Elijah found Elisha plowing in a field.

Elisha had no poverty mindset. He understood the principle of seed and harvest. That's why we find Elisha out in the field with 12 sets of oxen. He was an industrious, hardworking and faithful man. These are good qualities for someone who wants to prosper.

Elijah draped his mantle on Elisha while he worked. The young apprentice could have jumped up in the air and said, "Yes! I have the anointing! I'm the chosen one!" and ran off through the town proclaiming that he was the chosen prophet to take Elijah's place. If he would have done so, do you know what would have happened to him? Nothing! Elijah would have just gone back down to Wal-Mart, got him another mantle and kept on looking for his replacement.

There are three things that Elisha did that are important and connected to what we are talking about. That is, sowing into good soil and then reaping a multiplied blessing. Are you tired of having a pocketful of seeds and promises and prophetic words with no real blessing? Your promise will become a blessing and your prophetic word will become a reality when you release and sow your seed.

The Bible doesn't say this first point specifically, but it had to have taken place, because we know when Elijah took off in the chariot, his mantel fell to the ground. Therefore, after Elijah draped his mantle over the husky shoulders of Elisha, the young farmer must have taken it off and given it back to him. In other words, Elisha was saying, "I have been recognized but I have not been released. Here is the mantel back and when you are ready to send me, father, then you can give it back to me."

This was an acknowledgment of trust in the man of God. You can never sow your seed in faith if there is distrust for the recipient. This is why Satan works overtime to destroy the trust that congregants have in their pastors. If there is anything that steals the harvest of increase in many families, it is clear mistrust, division and sometimes hatred that they feel towards their leaders. It is short-circuiting the power flow of God's miraculous blessings.

The second thing that Elisha did that was significant was that he sowed into Elijah by serving him dinner. Do you see a pattern, yet? It seems like Elijah never had to cook his own meals! Between the birds, widows and farmers, he was well taken care of? Why?

Learning to Release

Because God saw to it that everyone that sowed into his life was immensely blessed. The Lord knew that Elijah was a walking farm field just waiting to receive, bless and multiply people's seeds. If you encounter such people, ask them if they are hungry. Ask them if they have any needs. Go find an offering plate. They might just be holding the keys to your destiny. They might just be the field that you have been looking for in order to sow your seed and find your increase.

The Bible says that Elisha killed the oxen, made a fire from the yoke, and he fixed steaks on the grill. He fixed food for Elijah. Elisha served Elijah. He sowed into his life a meal.

I have people call me and say, "I want you to mentor me, Pastor Mark. I want you to pour into me. I want your mantle." I'll say, "Good. Praise God. I will."

So I hang up the phone and I never call them. I never go see them. I never schedule an appointment. They call back in about three months and say, "Maybe you didn't understand me. I asked you to pour your life into me and to mentor me and you haven't done that yet."

"Okay."

I hang up the phone and I won't call them. I don't talk to them. I don't go and see them. Again the phone rings about three months later and they are angry and upset. I hear, "I have been waiting by the phone and you never call. I wait for a visit and you never came. I'm looking for someone else to mentor me. Good-bye!"

"Okay."

What I'm about to say may come as a surprise, but it is not my place to pursue a son. It is the place of a father to embrace the son, but it is the place of the son to pursue the father.

When Elijah started leaving, what did Elisha do? He ran after him. "You ain't leaving me, until I get that mantle back," he might have said. The third thing that Elisha did in order to get his harvest of increase was to follow the man of God and be consistent in his efforts.

Three times Elijah said, "Leave me alone."

Elisha said, "No, I ain't leaving."

"Get lost."

"No."

"You are bothering me, son."

"That's all right. I'm going to bother you until I get my harvest from that meal I served you. I am going to get what you got and I won't leave without it."

You see, I have found that God will put me in relationship with significant people who hold keys for my life. As I plant into them, it comes back to me multiplied. As I serve them, their mantle becomes available. In every case they do not pursue me but I pursue them. They don't serve me but I serve them. They do not sow into me but I sow into them. That's how I get my harvest!

Elisha got his double portion just like the widow got her blessing. They both released their seed into the fertile soil of the man of God. Thank God that neither suffered from a spirit of poverty that is afraid to release seed and give away resources as investments into the Kingdom of God.

REAPING A REWARD OF PEACE

Jesus sent out 70 disciples in Luke Chapter 10. They were supposed to go into the cities that Jesus was about to visit and they were to prepare those cities for His arrival. They were going to bless the people in those cities. Because of this, Jesus gave them some instructions. One of them was leave their billfolds behind. They were to take no provisions for themselves. They were to allow the families of these cities to sow into their lives. Like Elijah, God was sending good soil into these towns and villages and the people who invested their seeds into these Kingdom individuals would reap a great harvest.

"Put your billfolds down boys," Jesus said. "When you go to a city, I am going to have people in that city serve you and take care of you. You'll see. And whatever things they want to give you, receive them."

Now, I can imagine someone saying, "Oh but Jesus, I can't do that. I can't take from these helpless and poor families." This would have been my response. But Jesus instructed them to go into the city, knock on a door and say, "Jesus sent me here and you are supposed to house me, feed me and take care of my needs." I mean, this would be tough for me. Would it be hard for you to say those things? It is hard for us to receive, isn't it? I guarantee you that for most of us, it is tougher to receive than it is to give. It takes more humility to receive than it does to give most times. Have you ever washed somebody's feet? Have you ever had your own feet washed? Which takes more humility?

I used to think that the only reason why Jesus told them to leave their billfolds behind was to teach his disciples how to walk in faith. Although this was part of the reason, Verses 5, 6 and 7 reveal another reason why He wanted them to depend upon the people for their livelihood, "But whatever house you enter, first say, 'Peace to this house.' And if a son of peace is there, your peace will rest on it; if not, it will return to you. And remain in the same house, eating and drinking such things as they give, for the laborer is worthy of his wages."

Let me open up another door of possibility and suggest to you that the reason why Jesus did this was to allow the townspeople to sow their material seeds into the fertile lives of the men whom He had sent. He did this so that the families of those cities would be blessed with peace in preparation for His arrival. If the man of God takes his wallet and goes to McDonald's, he can get his hunger met and have himself a meal. But if the man of God is forced to knock on your door and come into your house and you fix him a meal, he gets his meal, and you get his blessing. That's cool!

I also used to look at that verse about eating whatever was fixed for you as a command to eat gross and disgusting things while being polite. I saw this as Jesus saying, "Boys, it's going to be rough. These ladies can't cook a lick and they fix horrible tasting food. But you've got to grin and bear it. Eat whatever spoiled and nasty food they give you." I was viewing this passage through the poverty lens. I naturally put a negative spin on the verse. It doesn't make sense that none of these people could cook. They were all from the same region and same culture. Rather, it's a command to allow people the privilege and opportunity to sow their material resources into the God-sent person so that entire households could be blessed and prospered.

With the natural mind, people may say, "Those preachers, all they want is my money." Not all preachers want your money - only the good ones! That is, those who understand that when you take care of their needs, then you and your household will be blessed. If you understand this principle, then how could you be upset about the opportunity to join the widow, Elisha and the townspeople in sowing seeds into the lives and ministries of people whom God has sent around the earth to advance His Kingdom?

If we could see how vital it is to recognize the opportunities to sow seeds into these fertile fields, we would shout for joy when the offering is taken. We would come early to church service when the missionaries are in town. We would dig up our talents and begin to sow them for a greater harvest. We would work harder, ask God for more and believe for increase and prosperity so we would have more seed to sow. That's why Paul said to the Corinthians in his second epistle to them in verse 10 of chapter 9, "Now may He who supplies seed to the sower, and bread for food, supply and multiply the seed you have sown and increase the fruits of your righteousness." The apostle saw the need to pray for greater seed in the hands of God's people in order to sow and reap a greater harvest. In this plan, everyone wins except the spirit of poverty!

DON'T BE AFRAID OF PROSPERITY

Because of our unwritten vow of poverty that we are all supposed to take when we get saved, many people are afraid of financial success. They feel guilty for being blessed. Having increase seems worldly and dangerous to them so they either shy away from success or they hide their blessings so no one will criticize them for having it. This misunderstanding needs to be put where it belongs: under our feet! It is the spirit of poverty that makes believers think this way and shields them from the full blessings of God.

Paul told his spiritual son, Timothy, in I Timothy 6:10, "For the love of money is a root of all kinds of evil..." Let this serve as a warning against all of those who do not tithe and give offerings! The only logical conclusion that a person can draw from someone who claims to be a believer and does not give back to the Lord God is that this person is a lover of money. Perhaps they also suffer from a spirit of poverty as well as walking in doubt and unbelief.

This verse says that the love of money is the root of all kinds of evil. It doesn't say money is the root of evil. It says the love of money is the root of all kinds of evil. Can I tell you that anything that we love more than God is a problem? So, yes, loving money more than God can lead us into all kinds of evil but so can loving your job more than God or loving sports more than God or loving your spouse more than God or loving your kids more than God, etc. Whatever you love more than God can be a root of all kinds of evil because it becomes idolatry. We usually worship at the shrine of those things that hold our passions and end up sacrificing to them instead of worshipping and sacrificing to God. That's why Jesus said that if you want to find out where a person's heart (passion) is, look for where they spend their money. "For where your treasure is, there your heart will be also (Matthew 6:21)."

Someone might look to the rich young ruler as a sign of how Jesus felt about being rich. Jesus instructed him to sell everything that he had and become a follower of Christ. What about him? Well, find one other place where Jesus required that from anyone else. He called his disciples to leave their boats and follow but not to sell them before they came. Trying to fit this unique story into more than this particular event with this particular man is not wise. That would be like saying that every person who wants to be healed has to have spit and mud placed into their eyes before they can see (see: John 9:6). Jesus saw the unique problems that this man's wealth was causing him. Jesus spoke to his idol and called him to become a disciple. He then instructed him to do what I have been suggesting to you in this book, use your wealth to advance the Kingdom of God. Giving is the only effective weapon when wealth and riches have become an idol in a person's life.

Learning to Release

Jesus told his disciples after being rejected by the rich young ruler that it is easier for a camel to go through the eye of a needle than it is for a rich man to enter the kingdom of God. The truth behind this statement is two-fold. First, we can see that it's easier to make a spiritual man wealthy than for a wealthy man to become spiritual. Secondly, a person must understand what the disciples knew when Jesus spoke about the eye of the needle. This was the name of a gate in Jerusalem where camels regularly traveled. Everybody that heard him talk about the eye of the needle knew that he wasn't talking about that thing with thread running through it but was referring to this very low entrance into the marketplace. In order for a camel to go through this small gate, they had to unpack their load and bend to their knees. This is a picture of what Jesus expects of every believer who follows him. We must give our resources for the advancement of His Kingdom and we must bow the knee to His Lordship and Ownership of all our wealth and of us.

People who point to the story of the rich young ruler as evidence that Jesus does not like wealth and riches forget to read the conclusion of the event in Mark chapter 10. When Peter reminded Jesus that they had left everything to follow their Messiah, Jesus promised them in verses 29 and 30, "Assuredly, I say to you, there is no one who has left house or brothers or sisters or father or mother or wife or children or lands, for My sake and the gospel's, who shall not receive a hundredfold now in this time--houses and brothers and sisters and mothers and children and lands, with persecutions--and in the age to come, eternal life."

Jesus promised two things in this passage that pertain to the subject of this writing. First, He promised increase and prosperity for those who walk in obedience. Secondly, He promised that persecutions would follow those who are blessed. Many of these persecutions will undoubtedly come from those who are influenced by those first cousin spirits, poverty and religion.

As we have said before, many people are successful but there is something greater than success. It is significance. You will find significance when you understand the purpose behind wealth. The purpose behind wealth is not to make your life easier. It is to advance the kingdom. I believe with all of my heart that across the world God is raising up kingdom-minded people that He will bless tremendously to transfer wealth from the wicked to the righteous, from the kingdoms of this world to the Kingdom of God. These men and woman are going to be like camels at the eye of the needle; they are going to know how to lay their wealth down and they are going to be people that are submitted and on their knees. I want you to become one of those people!

BECOME THE GOOD SAMARITAN

Before we leave this subject of learning how to release, let me lay a challenge before you. I want you to begin praying that you will become a Good Samaritan. We often hear about the love and compassion in action when this man helped the poor, beaten traveler. We scoff at the priest and Levite passing by on the other side. Undoubtedly, they could have had more compassion for this poor fellow. But have you ever thought that the reason why they passed by on the other side is because they felt like they couldn't afford to help the man? I wonder if they saw him through the poverty lens and felt like his need was too great for their resources?

Here's an important question: How many of us could afford to be the Good Samaritan? How many of us could have taken care of the injured man like the Samaritan took care of him? He paid all of this man's health care and living expenses with room and board for several days if not weeks. If you gave someone a room in a local hotel, let them order room service three times a day, bought medicine and paid a nurse to care for him, you could expect to pay about $2,500 a week. How many of us don't even bring that much money home to our families in a month?

There are millions of beaten and injured people just like this man in the world today. They are waiting, not for more priests and Levites to bless their mess, but for people who can create wealth and release it at the eye of the needle, wealth that can be used to help these hurting people and advance the Kingdom of God. Are you ready?

CHAPTER 8

"Farmers, Seeds and Soil"

Paul admonished Timothy in II Timothy 2:6 to emulate "the hard-working farmer" who, after planting his seed, "must be first to partake of the crops." The emphasis here is on the hard work that precedes the reaping of the crop. Part of that hard work is planting the seed. The first step in receiving your harvest is investing your seed. You've got to start thinking like a farmer. The farmer plants with a purpose in mind. He plants with the expectation of harvest. He understands that soil was made for seed and seed for soil. If he is going to have a harvest, he must look for these two things: Good seed and good soil.

YOUR SEED WAS MADE FOR SOWING

What God wants to do in your life financially is irrevocably tied to the seed that you plant. You cannot get away from that. God wants to release abundance upon you and your family but first you must posture yourself for that blessing. The blessings of God in your life will come to you as fruit that you have reaped. That fruit is directly connected with the planting of your seed. You can talk about

Farmers, Seeds and Soil

fruit all you want, but you're not going to have any until you plant that seed that's in your hand.

Anytime we talk about releasing your seed, you have a choice to make. You can either look at your seed or look at your need. The devil will try to convince you that you have too many needs in your life to invest your seed. He will convince you that if you give it away, you will never get it back. Your kids will go hungry, the bank will repossess the family home and you will become a failure. In reality, however, the opposite is true.

God promised Noah that as long as mankind was alive on the earth, there would be seedtime and harvest (Genesis 8:22). This natural law is a mirror image of the spiritual law that Paul spoke about in II Corinthians 9:6 when he was encouraging the Corinthians to give in his offering. He said, "But this I say: He who sows sparingly will also reap sparingly, and he who sows bountifully will also reap bountifully."

We can see clearly from the above passages that God's blessings come in the form of a harvest that has grown from the seeds we have sown. Satan knows this. In order to keep you living a fruitless life, he assigns the spirit of poverty to make you afraid to give, focusing on your need instead of your seed. In time, you will eat more and more of the seeds you should be investing for future harvest. Seeds were made for planting, not just eating. Therefore, God's future blessings in your life start with the seed that is presently in your hand.

The miracle of the resurrection of Jesus started as a seed that was sowed. When speaking of His future suffering and glorious resurrection, Jesus said, "Most assuredly, I say to you, unless a grain of wheat falls into the ground and dies, it remains alone; but if it dies, it produces much grain (John 12:24)." If you are a Christian, you are part of His harvest. He had you in mind when He allowed Himself to be put into the ground like a seed. Anytime we talk about salvation by the resurrection of Jesus Christ, we are talking about an event that is traced back to the principle of seed sowing. All life begins with a seed. We cannot talk about being saved or even our own families without acknowledging the abilities of a seed to multiply.

Seeds were created to multiply and bring forth life. I saw this truth firsthand not long after we paved our parking lot at church. I was walking across it and saw something that caught my eye. A weed was growing through a very small crack in the pavement. I was amazed. I stood over the crack and thought about the power of the seed. Somehow, someway, that little seed found the smallest of cracks in that blacktop and fell inside. The power and life of that seed burst forth and not even the asphalt could stop it from multiplying. We have got to learn the lesson of the seed if we ever expect to break the spirit of poverty and walk in abundance. Seeds were made for planting!

If you were a farmer and wanted to increase your harvest, what would you do? I will tell you. There are two things you would have to do in order to increase your harvest. First, you would have to find bigger fields. Secondly, you would have to sow more seed. Easy, isn't it? You can have a lot of seed but no ground and you are not going to have a harvest. You can have a lot of ground but no seed and you're not going to have a harvest. You have got to have both in order to have a bigger harvest.

GOOD SOIL

Simply put, the ministry of the Church is the ground. Your financial support of it is the seed. When you go to work everyday and wealth is transferred to you through a check that you pick up every

Farmers, Seeds and Soil

two weeks, that's your seed. The Church can provide good ground and you can provide the seed. When the two are introduced to one another, your harvest begins.

You need to be warned at this point not to sow your seed in bad soil. Don't go to the desert to sow your seed. Go find a place where things are already growing and plant your seed there. News flash! Where there is nothing growing, there is probably a reason for it. What unfortunately happens with many people is that they sow their seed more out of sympathy rather than faith. They pay their tithes to a place that is fruitless because they feel sorry for it. People who insist on giving their tithe out of sympathy into a barren ground are not abundantly blessed because they are not sowing in fruitful soil. How much sense would it make if a farmer felt sorry for the Sahara Desert and said, "C'mon Delores, let's go over there to that desert and sow our seed into that soil. It really looks like it needs our help." Another news flash! There are reasons why nothing grows in a desert! The smart farmer looks for a place that's already producing something as a good location to sow his seed. Wisdom dictates that if you want to find a place where your seed is going to multiply, find a place of life where there are disciples being made. That's good soil.

Just as a farmer needs seed and soil, the responsibility of the church is to provide a place for people to sow their seed. Pastors and church leaders should have a vision that creates good soil and stimulates life. They need to be evangelizing the lost, changing their communities, making disciples, experiencing the presence of God in worship, sending out people to minister to others, etc. When you find a place like that, start sowing seed. It's a privilege and honor to find such a place if you are a farmer looking for a harvest. That's why pastors should never apologize for creating opportunities for people to sow their seed.

Unfortunately, most pastors feel guilty for receiving offerings. They have been criticized for talking too much about money. When they do approach the subject, they feel the collective withdraw from their congregation when the ushers are called forward. It should not be that way. Think about this: If everyone in a congregation had a 10-pound bag of seed and needed somewhere to sow it in order to take care of their families and the pastor had a 200-acre farm with beautiful soil that was ready for that seed, why should he or she apologize for giving the people an opportunity to plant their seeds in this land? Wouldn't it be silly to criticize the man or woman of God for giving you ground to sow your seed into? Yes it would! We must see our resources as seed and the ministries of the church as soil. When the two meet, there is multiplication.

The job of the church is to create good soil. A visionary in the church is someone who will see a vision, dream a dream, clear the land and plow the field. He or she will have the fresh dark soil turned over for you to enjoy. There will be a sign placed out front saying, "Seeds Needed!" The visionary will then believe that God is going to bring people to plant seed in this ground. Together, they can partake of an abundant harvest. But if the devil can get you to eat your seed, distrust the person who is offering the ground or foolishly plant your seed in the desert, you will never walk in abundance. Don't eat your seed, don't plant it foolishly or cease from trusting your leaders.

Someone might be saying right now, "Oh but Pastor Mark, I heard about a TV preacher who took millions from little old ladies." Yes, that's probably right. There probably have been people who have unfortunately done this. The same could be true for athletes but does that stop you from watching the World Series or Super Bowl? The same could be said about retailers or grocers but does that stop you from buying clothes and food? The same could be said about many politicians but does that keep you from voting? It shouldn't. Neither should a scandal involving a greedy and selfish man or woman of God keep you from investing your seed. Remember, if there is a counterfeit, that means that there is a genuine somewhere!

At some point in time trust is a two-way street. You need to trust the leaders of the church in order for them to lead you and they need to trust that you will plant your seed in their vision in order to advance the Kingdom of God. If we can trust each other, great multiplication awaits us. If we cannot trust each other, Satan will continue to rob the church of her vision and the spirit of poverty will hold captive entire families, congregations and cities. He will work overtime to try and get people to mistrust the men and women of God that the Lord places in their lives. We cannot advance the Kingdom around the earth if there is no trust.

Someone will say, "Well, trust is earned." I've said that before, as well. But it's not quite right. Trust is an issue of faith, not works. Just like investing your retirement money in an IRA, trust is an investment made into another person that empowers them to be in relationship with you. If you make everyone earn your trust, you're a manipulator. Instead of saying, "I will not trust you until you earn it," we should say, "I will trust you until you show me otherwise." See the difference?

In the Kingdom of God trust is not earned, it is invested. It is not based upon the works of the individual but it is based upon the commands of the Lord Jesus Christ who saves and forgives us all. Investing trust in your spiritual leaders is an act of faith that God rewards. It is not based on their perfection, but in the call of God to work together and cover the earth with His Kingdom gospel. Any time you trust another human being, you do so in faith. In order for the Kingdom of God to go anywhere, there must be times when we say, "Pastor, I trust you."

Anytime we take it upon ourselves to set the standard for another human being to achieve in order to earn our trust, we are not only manipulating them but we have set ourselves up as god. Who gave us the right to set the standard, anyway? Who created the test that sets the passing grade for people to earn trust? Where did we get our standards? Are we willing for God to use the same standards for us in order to earn His favor? I don't know about you, but I need grace in order to receive from God. If I need it from Him, shouldn't I extend it to others? If God's investment into us is not earned, then why should we expect others to earn our investment of trust? Let's begin to act in faith and invest our trust into our leaders based upon the fact that God in His mercy has saved us and called us to spread the gospel. Let's sow our seed without strings attached. Let's put them under the ground and watch them disappear under the dark, rich soil of the church. In a few months, the harvest will begin.

THE FARMER

If dirt could talk, what would it say? It probably would say something like, "Give it to me!" People with a poverty mindset have a greater connection with the dirt than they do the farmer. They see themselves as having nothing and in need of everything. When asked for an offering, they are the ones who say, "Give you something? You ought to be giving me something!" Aren't you glad that the widow woman didn't say that to Elijah when he asked for her last meal? People with a poverty mindset relate more with being dirt than they do with being a farmer because they see themselves in lack. They feel as if they are void of any seed to sow and the best that they can hope for is that someone will invest in them because, according to their thinking, they could never do it for themselves. That's why they remain for two or three generations on the welfare rolls. That's why they don't go to college. That's why they don't get a job. Over and over again the poverty spirit robs them of their ability to become a farmer.

What is a farmer? The farmer is one that says, "I have seed and I'm going to sow it." They understand that what's in their hand is the down payment of their harvest. When a farmer sees a seed, he does not see a meal but a harvest. He understands that investing that seed into his own stomach is ultimately going to cost him a thousand times more than the single kernel he just ingested. While people who think like dirt say, "Give it to me," a farmer says, "I'm going to give it away."

The spirit of poverty will destroy your self- confidence so that you don't have enough faith in yourself to ever feel like a farmer. That overwhelming sense of lack will always keep you thinking like dirt, always looking for someone to give you a handout. All the while, you are full of seeds that are waiting to be planted. Satan wants you to believe that you could never do it for yourself. He and his demons are working overtime to get you to buy the lie that you are helpless. He wants you to adopt the identity of a victim who is always on the losing end of life. He wants you to believe that the only way you will ever make it in life is to steal somebody else's money, win the lottery, have a rich uncle die and leave you an inheritance or latch yourself onto the government and let it pay all your bills for the rest of your life. Dirt never feels better than that!

But farmers do! They see themselves as having something worthwhile. They see themselves as valuable because they have learned the potential of the seed. While everyone else sees a little seed, they see a tree! While everyone else is busy doing nothing, they are busy preparing the ground. A farmer sees the field and the harvest at the same moment in time. He understands that he doesn't have to be perfect in order for the seed to grow. He doesn't have to measure up to everyone else's standards for the harvest to come to fruition. The farmer understands his worth apart from the seed but he also sees his great potential with the seed. He knows that his ability to gain a harvest is more dependant upon Gods promises than it is upon himself.

The spirit of poverty wants to rob you of this thrill. Satan wants to keep that seed in your possession, or better yet, buried in your backyard. He doesn't want you to think like a farmer. He wants to rob you of the ability to sow your seed by convincing you that you could never be that powerful, you could never be that wealthy, you could never be that independent, you could never be that prosperous and you could never be that successful. He will tell you that the only thing that you will ever amount to is a piece of dirt that needs others to sow into you in order to survive.

Our youth pastor talked to the elders of our church a few months after he arrived and began working with our teens. He said, "One thing I noticed about the teenagers around here, none of them believe in themselves. One will say, 'Well, I want to go into the medical field.' Then I will say, 'Oh, great, you are going to be a doctor?' Then they will say, 'No, I could never do that. Maybe I could be a nurse's aid, or maybe I could be a lab tech or something, but I could never be a doctor. I can never achieve that.'"

He then said he would talk to one teen after another about their dreams and plans for life and they would say, "I would love to be a university professor. But I know that I'm not smart enough." Another teen would say something like, "Wow, wouldn't it be great to be a lawyer? But I know that I could never go that far." On and on it went. "No, I could never be an engineer... I could never be a senator...I could never be a judge." It struck him as being something uniquely strong in our area of the country. I'll tell you what it is. It is the spirit of poverty!

The spirit of poverty is working on these young people, stealing their ambitions and dreams, leaving them full of self-doubt and unbelief. It has convinced them, even at a young age, that the best that they can do is bury their talent in their backyard and not lose it.

Don't you think it's time to change all of that? Don't you think it's time to begin believing in ourselves again? Don't you think that the next generation deserves a fighting chance? I do! And it is happening. What a joy it was for me to sit on the front row of the church I pastor and see about 20 young people, including my son, standing before our congregation. These were some of the same kids that our youth pastor talked about earlier. We are working hard to release a generation of world-changers on the earth. Each one was asked about their future plans. One after another said things like, "I'm going to such-and-such university to become an engineer...I will be in pre-med...I want to be a carpenter...I am majoring in business...I am going to study how to make movies...I am going to study law...I want to be a math teacher..." Not one spoke under the influence of a spirit of poverty!

CHAPTER 9

"Four Types of Giving"

To move from thinking like dirt to a farmer, you need to stop thinking about how much you want your harvest to be and start looking at how much seed you have. In other words, stop saying, "Boy, it would be great to have a million dollars" and start looking at what you do have in your hand. Quit saying, "Gee, it would be great to be able just to write a $10,000 check and give it to a missionary" and start writing a check for the amount that you can give. Today it might only be $10.00. Making statements about what you wish you could do is like a farmer standing in the field with seed in his hand saying, "Boy, wouldn't it be great if this whole field was full of corn." If you want the harvest, start sowing your seed. Instead of wasting your time dreaming about millions of dollars and even tens of thousands of dollars, start living where you're at and deal with the ten dollars that you held back from God when you were given the last opportunity to give.

Our problem is that we want a million dollar harvest with a one-dollar seed. When we are in trouble we're crying out for a million dollar miracle but when it's time to give our seed, we start looking for

Four Types of Giving

the one-dollar bills. The worst nightmare of a stingy person is when the offering is being taken and he or she has no one-dollar bills in the wallet. People will bypass the tens and twenties to get to the ones. When the ushers move forward, it's almost automatic, "How many ones have I got in there? Oh, there is a twenty, there is a ten, there are two fives. Oh, thank God. There is a one-dollar bill. Hallelujah!"

I want to ask you something: When you need a miracle of God for your sick children, wayward grandchildren or a dying loved one, are you asking for a million dollar blessing or a one-dollar crumb? Are we asking for God's best when we need a breakthrough but when it comes time for us to take a step in faith and sow our seed, we become stingy? I wonder.

Wouldn't you like to see the face of that missionary light up when you slide a $10,000 check across the table and say, "Go ahead, build that orphanage?" I would. Maybe you haven't written a $10,000.00 check, a $1,000.00 check or even a $100.00 check yet, but you are going to! From there, you are going to be able to plant a $100,000 seed and then you're going to go to the next level and give away $1,000,000 for the work of the Kingdom of God around the world.

I know, I know. We are talking about some big numbers here and I can imagine the spirit of poverty is screaming at you saying, "No way! That's never going to happen. You will never be able to do that." Satan wants to steal your dream right now. He wants to pull you back into the backyard, hand you a shovel and say, "Start digging, slave!" He wants you to believe that the only hope you will ever have for survival is to bury your treasure so you won't lose it. But other people reading this book are going to start believing the Bible and believing in themselves. They are going to believe that God wants to bless them and has given them an inheritance so they can abundantly bless other people and advance the Kingdom of God. Which one are you?

Here is where I want to challenge you: Whenever you sow your seed, be as generous with your stuff as much as you need for God to be generous with His stuff. Why? Because the Bible says that you will reap what you sow (Luke 6:38; II Corinthians 9:6; Galatians 6:9). What if God treated us like we treat the offering? What if He gave to us with the same attitude that we give to Him? What if, when you asked from Him, He looked through His blessings like we look through our wallets? He would bypass all of the twenties, tens and fives and find the smallest answer He could provide for you. Is that what you want from God? Then why do we think it's any different when we give to God, not our best, but our least? Shouldn't we be planting our best if we want our harvest from God to be its best?

I want to challenge you to dream bigger! I want to challenge you to become a hilarious giver like Paul talked about in II Corinthians 9:7. I want to challenge you to begin to add 0's to whatever you normally give. If you are a one-dollar person, become a ten-dollar person. If you are a ten-dollar person become a hundred-dollar person. If you are a hundred-dollar person, become a thousand-dollar person. If you are a thousand-dollar person, become a ten thousand dollar person. Where do you stop? You decide!

TITHES

The first type of giving that the Bible speaks of is the tithe. Tithe is ten percent of your income. Income by its definition sometimes can be called your increase. The reason that this is important for some people is because if they are business owners, their increase is their profit margin. Once they pay for their suppliers and pay their employees, at the end of the week, they may have a five percent profit from the total amount of income. They may have made $200,000 of gross income that week, but their increase was $10,000. Of that increase, the first 10% belongs to God. If that business owner will recognize God in his increase, God will bless that business. He promised that He would. "'Bring all the tithes into the storehouse, that there may be food in My house. And try Me now in this,' Says the LORD of hosts, 'If I will not open for you the windows of heaven and pour out for you such blessing that there will not be room enough to receive it (Malachi 3:10).'" If you are a business owner, that should excite you.

If you are like most Americans who get a paycheck, the amount you are required to tithe on would be what you are making as a salary. Don't do what I have heard that some people do. They will bring home a paycheck, take out the car payment, house payment, electric bill, etc., and what little bit they have left over, they pay ten percent of that. That is not your tithe. That's robbery. God said in Malachi 3:8, "Will a man rob God? Yet you have robbed Me! But you say, 'In what way have we robbed You?' In tithes and offerings." There's no mistaking that language.

Now, let me cover something right here. Somebody who wants to get out of paying tithe will protest, "Wait just a minute Pastor Mark. Isn't tithing part of the Old Testament Law? We don't live by the law so I don't have to tithe." First, what kind of a person does it take to find ways not to be generous? You can answer that question. Second, what farmer would complain about planting their seed today because that's what they did in the Old Testament? I'll answer that one for you: A stupid one! Thirdly, and most importantly, anyone who says that tithing is only an issue of the Law needs to read their Bible. Abraham gave tithe to Melchizedek 500 years BEFORE the Law was written. No, tithing is not an issue of the Law; it's an issue of the covenant. It connects us with Abraham like Paul said in Genesis 3:29, "And if you are Christ's, then you are Abraham's seed, and heirs according to the promise."

Every Jew understood and obeyed the tithing requirement, even Jesus. He affirmed the tithing practices of the Pharisees and encouraged them to add to their obedience of the word of God to other important issues. In Matthew 23:23 He said, "These you ought to have done (tithe), without leaving the others (justice, mercy and faith) undone."

Any believer that says that they have faith in God and does not tithe is just blowing smoke. How can we say that we are trusting God with everything we have and not give God what belongs to Him? When people do not tithe, they are stating a fact. They are saying that they trust themselves to handle that 10% more than they trust God to handle it. It feels safer in their hands than it does in God's hands.

The Bible makes it clear that tithing is not an option. I can think of no other reason for a believer not to tithe except for a lack of faith and greediness. I don't know about you, but I do not want to be associated with either of those qualities.

Somebody may ask whether they should tithe before taxes or after taxes? My question is this: How generous do you want to be? Or more importantly, how generous do you want God to be? Do you want Him to bless you before or after taxes? A generous person would never ask a question like that. A generous person is not looking for ways NOT to give; they are looking for new and exciting ways TO give. Wives, would you want your husbands looking for new and unusual ways to get out of giving you Christmas presents? Husbands, answer the same question. When you love someone and want to express it, you don't look for the imaginative loopholes to get out of giving, do you? If you do, I would question your love. Is that

Four Types of Giving

the kind of person you want to become? I don't think so. You look for ways to show your love, don't you? Does God deserve any less?

You have to see that you are planting seeds for your harvest when you give. So if you are going to fudge either way, don't fudge on being a cheapskate. Let's say that you get a paycheck and at the end of the week your tithe is $58.90. Don't make the check for that exact amount like some Pharisee trying to do just enough to stay religious. Don't be the type of person who does just enough to barely survive spiritually. Be generous! Why not just round it up to $60.00. Or better yet, add an extra 10% to that amount and give God a double blessing. Have you ever needed a double blessing? Don't be the type of person that's going to do barely enough. If you do, then you will be a "barely-enough" believer serving a "barely-enough" God and winning "barely-enough" victories.

Do you see the spirit of poverty all over that?

Look in Malachi chapter three to see what will happen to you if you become a tither. The tithe has blessings all over it! If you want these blessings, they are there for the taking!

(1) First, the windows of Heaven will be open.

You will have an open window to the blessings of Heaven.

(2) Secondly, your barns will not contain the blessings.

That means you are going to start harvesting your blessing.

(3) Thirdly, the devourer is rebuked.

This would lead me to believe that there is a demon spirit assigned to devour the finances of those people who are robbing from God. Why? Because this passage says if you are not a tither you are robbing from God. Do you ever feel that you are making more than enough money to survive but you are still going under? This may be the work of the devourer.

(4) Finally, people will call you blessed.

You will have a testimony. People are going to see that you are a blessed individual and they will come to you and ask advice. They are going to want to know your "secret." At that point, you can tell them what has made you so blessed!

FIRSTFRUITS

The second type of giving is very much like the first. It is called firstfruits. This is a spontaneous and generous gift that is given to God from an unexpected bonus of income. When you become a tither, you can expect these unexpected blessings! They will come to you from various places. Jesus said, "Give, and it will be given to you: good measure, pressed down, shaken together, and running over will be put into your bosom. For with the same measure that you use, it will be measured back to you (Luke 6:38)." When these blessings return to us from unexpected places, we have even more opportunities to sow our seed.

These firstfruit offerings are in recognition of God's blessings. It is a statement, over and above your tithe, that God is your source and that you love Him supremely. For instance, I know a business owner that gives away the first paycheck of every new contract they sign. I know other people who give tithe before taxes, and when they get their income tax return, they give God the first 10% of that, even though they have already tithed on that money. I know another person who gives God their first paycheck at the beginning of every New Year. Another man gives all of the profits of the first car he sells every month.

Four Types of Giving

Why do these people do this? Because they are showing their love to the Lord and giving recognition that He is their source. Are you going to tell me that God won't bless those people? Sure He will – abundantly! This type of love and generosity from His children blesses our Father in heaven. When Israel would harvest the new grain, they would bring the first part to God and give it to Him. This was their firstfruit and God would bless them for it. The people whom I just mentioned are doing the same.

I heard a story once when I was still in Bible College. The guest speaker was a congressman who told us about his son when they went to McDonald's to get a Happy Meal. His son opened up his Happy Meal and started munching on the french-fries. The dad didn't think he was hungry until he smelled those fries and saw his child devouring them. He leaned over and said, "Son, let me have one of these French-fries." That little boy took those French-fries and pulled them away saying, "No, my French-fries!"

At that point the man telling the story said that God began to speak to him. He said, "Take a look at your son because that's what people do to me." There are three facts about that French-fry story that the father learned. First, all of those French-fries were given to the boy by his father and, by all rights, all the fries belonged to him. Secondly, the father is big enough to take all of those French-fries if he so desires. Thirdly, it is in the son's best interest to surrender a few fries to his father!

Likewise, it is in our best interest to give to God the firstfruits of our blessings. How much better would it have been if that son had looked at his father without being asked and said, "Hey dad, want the first one? They're really are hot and good!" That father and son would have shared more than French-fries, they would have shared a moment. Forevermore, their relationship would have been deeper and stronger. Besides this, the father would have gladly given his son a lifetime supply of french-fries!

Look at what the Bible says about the firstfruit offering:

"The firstfruits of your grain and your new wine and your oil, and the first of the fleece of your sheep, you shall give Him (Deuteronomy 18:4)."

"Honor the LORD with your possessions, And with the firstfruits of all your increase; So your barns will be filled with plenty, And your vats will overflow with new wine (Proverbs 3:9-10)."

"The best of all firstfruits of any kind, and every sacrifice of any kind from all your sacrifices, shall be the priest's; also you shall give to the priest the first of your ground meal, to cause a blessing to rest on your house (Ezekiel 44:30)."

"For if the firstfruit is holy, the lump is also holy; and if the root is holy, so are the branches (Romans 11:16)."

In that last passage, Paul gives us the principle why the firstfruit offering is such a blessing. He reminds us that when the firstfruit is given to the Lord, the entire harvest is blessed. God showed Israel how to be blessed and as long as human beings have to feed their families and the Kingdom of God needs to advance over the earth, there is always going to be a need for people who sow and reap a financial blessing

ALMS

The third type of giving is alms. The motivation behind almsgiving is sympathy. You feel sorry for the poor so you give them something. The promise associated with almsgiving is that God will

Four Types of Giving

repay the amount that you give. The Book of Proverbs has a lot to say about almsgiving:

> "He who despises his neighbor sins; But he who has mercy on the poor, happy is he (Proverbs 14:21)."
>
> "He who has pity on the poor lends to the LORD, And He will pay back what he has given (Proverbs 19:17)."
>
> "Whoever shuts his ears to the cry of the poor will also cry himself and not be heard (Proverbs 21:13)."
>
> "He who gives to the poor will not lack, But he who hides his eyes will have many curses (Proverbs 28:27)."
>
> "For some thought, because Judas had the money box, that Jesus had said to him, "Buy those things we need for the feast," or that he should give something to the poor (John 13:29)."
>
> "They desired only that we should remember the poor, the very thing which I also was eager to do (Galatians 2:10)."

As you can see, every Christian needs to give to the poor. But not every offering should be a practice in almsgiving. We must not confuse almsgiving with the tithe and firstfruit offerings. Unfortunately, I believe that most offerings in churches are motivated through the almsgiving approach. You will find too many pastors using sympathy rather than faith to motivate their people to give. You hear things like, "People, we need your help tonight. We can't pay our bills. They are getting ready to shut the electric off. If you don't give tonight, I don't know what we are going to do. We may not even be open next week." They act like God is broke and reduce the Bride of Christ to a beggar on the street corner hoping for a coin to be tossed into her tin cup. Consequently, they are keeping their people from sowing seeds in faith and perpetually tying their offerings to almsgiving.

I was in a ministry one time where they had it all planned out. When the offering was called for, they turned all of the lights out in the building. It was totally dark. They said, "Would you want to come next week and find this? If you don't give, we can't make it." Can you see the spirit of poverty at work in that? You can never use poverty mindsets to break the spirit of poverty! People who give under such circumstances are being cheated of a greater harvest. They are being motivated out of sympathy and fear but are not sowing seeds in faith. They are lending to God and He will repay them as He said in Proverbs 19:17 but they are not being given the opportunity to exercise the necessary faith to see an abundant harvest.

Giving alms should be for the poor and not for the church. When people are moved with compassion for the poor, they should give. When they give to the church for the purpose of kingdom advancement, they should be challenged to give in faith and be told that it's an honor to give to the Lord in such a way. Remember, Abraham didn't give to Melchizedek because he needed Abraham's money. He was a king, himself. It was not for Melchizedek's benefit but for Abraham's benefit that God arranged this divine meeting. Let people know that it's a privilege to give to the church, not because the church is broke, but because God wants to bless the families in your congregation.

SEED SOWING

The fourth type of giving is seed-sowing. If the motivation behind tithing is obedience, the motivation behind firstfruits is love and the motivation behind almsgiving is sympathy, then the motivation behind seed-sowing is sheer faith. It is the superabundant and extravagant gift that defines the trust that a believer has in the

Four Types of Giving

abundance of God. It is the gift of faith that becomes specific. When a farmer plants beans, he expects to reap beans. When he plants corn, he expects to reap corn. Planting and harvesting is specific. When you sow a seed, tell God what your request is and step out in a wild faith that says, "God, I know this looks crazy, but here goes!"

A young couple was in my office this week getting ready to get married. The young husband-to-be is in college preparing for law school. His fiancée is almost done with her masters' degree. He said he was going to become an attorney and be a blessing to the Kingdom of God. Not long ago, he thought the only way he could serve God was to go to Bible College and be a minister of music. But God showed him that he could have greater influence as an attorney and still be a worshipper. Both he and his fiancée told me the same thing. They said, "Pastor, we want to be successful and prosperous because our goal one day is to live on the 10% and give away the 90%." Isn't that awesome? I believe that they will do it – and God bless the pastor in whose church they land!

Sowing a seed in this way is an act of faith that God blesses. No, you're not buying your blessing. Everyone knows that you can't do that! What is happening is that God is blessing people's faith as they give something so precious to them and needed to survive. We all need money to survive. Sowing a seed must be such a substantial amount of money that it makes it an act of faith by necessity.

Secondly, sowing a seed should be specific. A lady in our church found out firsthand about this. She came up to my wife, Nicki, and asked for prayer about a car. She said, "All I want is basic transportation."

Nicki asked, "Basic transportation, right?"

"Yes, that's it. All I need is basic transportation. I just need to get from point A to point B. I don't even care what it looks like"

BREAKING THE SPIRIT OF POVERTY

She sowed her seed and they agreed for basic transportation. Within 2 days she got her car. Someone gave her a car – and it was just what she asked for. It was basic transportation! Nothing extra. No frills. Basic transportation! She thanked God for it and then heard Him say, "Oh, if you would have asked me for more..."

Isn't that what Elisha told Joash in I Kings 13? He said to go strike the arrows on the ground and that's how you are going to strike the Syrians. And the king went over and tap, tap, tap, and the prophet said, "If you would have gone over there and hit the ground several times, you would have completely annihilated the Syrians, but because your faith was a tap-tap-tap faith, you're only going to defeat them three times and ultimately they are going to defeat you."

Be specific and full of faith when you sow your seed. Say, "God, I'm going to sow a seed for this and sow that seed in faith." Be specific about your request and don't allow the devil or religious people who have a poverty spirit to talk you out of it.

Also expect this: When you sow a significant seed in faith, you might feel really badly about an hour later. Hear me on this one! I am not talking about the times you put a dollar in the offering. I'm talking about the times you say to your spouse, "Honey, I know we can't afford this, but God said do it. Let's make a check out now." Once you do it, you feel great for about an hour. Then it hits you on the way home. Boom! "What have I just done?" At some point in time you are going to feel fearful and dreadful. The devil will jump on your back and tell you that you are going to go under and lose the farm because of this gift.

Remember Wile E. Coyote? He would run off the cliff and be okay for a while. Then he would look around and realized that he couldn't walk on air. When he did, he fell like a rock. That's exactly what Peter did. He made a faith step: "I can't walk on water!" He then

Four Types of Giving

asked himself, "What am I doing?" By the time he got an answer, down he went.

Faith is instantaneous, immediate, and bold. This type of giving reflects the type of faith that produces miracles. Just like Peter walking on water, doing something that he had not taken the time to talk himself out of yet, the giver of the faith seed discerns the season, hears the voice of God and jumps out of the boat. That's why it initiates such a miraculous blessing from heaven.

Friend, I'm telling you, until you start sowing your seed of faith, until you start thinking better than dirt and bigger than dollar bills, you will never see the miraculous provision of God in your life. Start thinking like a farmer and begin looking for good soil into which your seed can be sown. It is the place where you will find your greatest reward!

CHAPTER 10

"Why Do Preachers Talk About Money All the Time?"

Can I answer that question? Because they want you blessed!

Anyone with any sense of honesty will have to admit that they are concerned about their financial status. When do we think about money? When the kids go off to college, when the bills need paid, when the paycheck is received, when the kids need school clothes, when the son-in-law loses his job, when the social security check is late, when we need groceries, when the pay raise is offered, when the credit card is racking up, when the bank is calling, when the gas prices rise, when the car breaks down... Need I go on? We think about money issues everyday of our lives. It's no wonder that Jesus spoke more about money issues than any other one issue in the Bible.

How we handle our money is especially important for Americans. The spirit of poverty should never intimidate preachers and teachers in America to shy away from talking about financial issues from the pulpit. No matter how many greedy people may be angered, there are still enough honest and hungry people in the pews to make the truth worth preaching. I believe that there are millions of willing and hungry people waiting for this revelation.

THREE KEY REASONS WHY AMERICANS NEED TO UNDERSTAND THE PRINCIPLES OF GIVING

There are three key reasons why Americans need to hear their ministers talk about money in the church. First, the Bible says in Luke 12:48, "...for everyone to whom much is given, from him much will be required; and to whom much has been committed, of him they will ask the more." Simply put, God's expectation of American Christians will be more because we have been blessed with so much more than the rest of the world. God has blessed America. He gave us these blessings, however, not to heap them upon ourselves but for the purpose of releasing it to advance the Kingdom of God around the earth. If a person or church is not doing that, then they are not walking in God's purposes for these financial blessings.

The verse that precedes the above passage is crucial for understanding the context in which Jesus uttered this truth. It said, "And that servant who knew his master's will, and did not prepare himself or do according to his will, shall be beaten with many stripes." Jesus is reminding us that in the end, we are all going to be judged according to the amount of blessings that we were given by God. If that's true, then Americans will be judged very strictly. We are the wealthiest society that has ever lived on this planet. God's criteria for judgment will largely be based upon how we handled these tremendous blessings. If that's the case, don't you think that teachers and preachers should be saying more about money without feeling intimidated and apologetic?

The second reason why Americans need to hear about money is because it is a stronghold and powerful demonic influence in our nation. Some would even say that greed is the strongman of the United States of America. Idols such as this in a nation need to be spoken against by the men and women of God. The Bible tells us in James 4:7 that we are to resist the devil. That word resist in its original language was a wrestling term that meant to push in the opposite direction. When Americans are giving to the Lord in an offering, they are resisting that spirit of mammon and that spirit of greed. Whenever pastors receive an offering, they are allowing the congregation to put works to their faith and come against these demonic strongholds in our nation. Giving into offerings is an act of incredibly effective spiritual warfare.

The third reason why we need to talk more about money in the church is that for most American Christians, the only place where they practice faith is when they are giving into the offering. Think about it, how many times do you really have to do something in faith other than bring your tithe check to the storehouse? In what other ways do we consistently have to act in faith in America?

Unlike the early church and many of our brothers and sisters around the world who have to assemble every week in faith, Americans worship freely. Unlike other people who have to trust God for every meal and walk in faith for shelter at night, most Americans never give it a second thought when they come home from work at the end of the day. In fact, the average American spends more money trying to figure out how to stop eating and lose weight than they spend every year feeding those people who are starving worldwide.

Learning the principles outlined in this book will give you the necessary truth to step out in faith and begin seeing miracles take place in your life. Never forget what the Bible says: "But without faith it is impossible to please Him, for he who comes to God must believe that He is, and that He is a rewarder of those who diligently seek Him (Hebrews 11:6)." Releasing and giving up what our nation worships is a huge spiritual activity that requires faith and assures us that we can be at peace before God and confidant at the appearing of our Lord Jesus Christ.

HARVEST IS HARD WORK

We know that faith without works is what? Dead! James repeats this fact twice in his epistle (2:20 and 26). It's not enough just to believe God's word. James tells us that even demons believe and they tremble (2:19). So we don't just believe God's word, we act upon it. When we talk about believing God's word and breaking the Spirit of Poverty, we're not just talking about putting money in an offering and then sitting back to receive the harvest. We must add works to our faith. Otherwise faith is dead.

Just today I was visiting a friend's restaurant, which just opened about three weeks ago. We had just completed our meal and people were standing in line to be served. God has blessed their business tremendously. When they began, they moved beyond a poverty mindset, stepped out in faith and sowed seed generously. While most people would have been saving every nickel and pinching every penny, they were sowing seeds everywhere they could. When they opened up their business, they met their 6 month projected budget in just 3 weeks! People from the corporate office were amazed at their success as they were setting new records for themselves.

As we sat there enjoying our food, my friend looked at me and said, "Harvesting is hard work."

I said, "What do you mean?"

He said, "We have been working hard in this place harvesting all of the seeds that we have been planting. It's hard work being blessed!"

At that moment I remembered working in the hayfields when I was a boy. In the springtime, my dad might sit on his tractor and spread some seed on the ground and top it off with some fertilizer (made fresh from the cows in the barn!). Seed sowing was always the easy part. In a few weeks, however, he would have all of us kids in the heat of the day bailing the hay that had grown. This was our harvest. It never really occurred to me until my friend said something but harvesting the hay and storing it in the barn was, by far, the hardest work of the year.

Don't look for your harvest in the mailbox. Don't look for your harvest under the gray matter that gets scratched off on the lottery ticket. Don't wait around until someone hands you your harvest. Invest your seed and then begin to work for your harvest. God blesses those people who understand that it takes both faith AND works. Your harvest may come as a new job offer. It may come in the way of investment opportunities. It may come as a part-time job prospect. Perhaps God will give you a witty invention or an idea that can create a business or a new product line in a store. Wealth is gained through power (Deuteronomy 8:18) and is accumulated over time and with much wisdom and hard work. If you are willing to obey God's word and work hard, God will begin to bless your life and you will escape the spirit of poverty.

SEVEN BLESSINGS ON THE GIVER

We started this chapter asking the question, why do preachers talk about money all the time. The answer is simple: Because they want you blessed! Here are seven blessings that I have observed over the years that follow those people who are obedient and generous with their wealth.

(1) People who give generously receive unexpected blessings.

Some of those unexpected blessings include the ever famous "check in the mail" but usually comes in the form of bonuses from work, job offers, gifts from loved ones, sales opportunities, key relationships, etc. They may come in the form of money or in another form like help on a project, advice for being successful, new leads for potential sales, new stock items for your store or needed manpower at just the right time.

I can't tell you the times that Nicki and I have been blessed in such ways. Just a couple of weeks ago friends of ours were moving and decided that their sofa did not fit their new décor. It was one of those sofas that have a pullout bed inside. They asked if we could use it and we said, "Sure." We had a bonus room over our garage that needed some furniture. A day or two after we received the sofa, we had a college intern move into our bonus room for the summer to do work in our church. He needed a place to sleep and the sofa bed came at just the right time.

(2) People who give generously find incredible bargains.

When someone gives God His 10%, He will bless the remaining 90%. When you become a substantial giver, you might find that you are not paying retail for anything. My wife will tell you, she finds incredible bargains all the time. When she comes home carrying all kinds of shopping bags, she'll say, "Mark, come over here and look at all of the money I saved us." I still haven't figured out that kind of math yet but I'm trying! I think it's a girl thing!

(3) People who give generously walk in greater victory.

I have never met a victorious, overcoming Christian that was not a giver. They have all been tithers and believe heavily in seed sowing. Their generosity and liberality runs both ways. They can give and receive with equal enthusiasm. Their faith has pleased God and defeated the enemy. They have opened up the windows of heaven with their giving and are experiencing great spiritual breakthroughs because of it.

On the other hand, I have never met someone who was stingy with his or her money and refused to tithe that ever walked in great victory. Their spiritual journey is nominal at best and usually marked with stagnation and fruitlessness. Their disposition is normally numb to the things of God and controlled by the spirit of this world. How could it be any different? In order not to tithe and give offerings, a person has to be willing to live in continual rebellion against God and justify why they are able to rob from Him every Sunday.

(4) People who give generously know God in deeper ways.

Most people can quote John 3:16. It says that "For God so loved the world that he GAVE His only begotten son..." We are never more like God than when we give. When a person gives their best, they are living in the spirit of John 3:16 and are becoming more and more Christ-like with each gift that they deposit. Because of this, they can relate with God with a clear conscience, unlike Adam and Eve who hid from Him after sinning. Do you know why people who give generously know God in deeper ways? Because every Sunday they are obeying His word, trusting him in faith and becoming more and more like Him. Either fear or faith will define a person's relationship with God. Opportunities to give are opportunities to either move towards God or away from Him. When Peter was walking on the water, he was stepping out in obedience and faith. People who give generously feel the same way.

(5) People who give generously live in greater satisfaction.

When you release what belongs to God, you have dealt with the spirit of idolatry, greed and the spirit of mammon that eats away at our contentment. Have you ever noticed that the more you get, the more you want; that people who accumulate wealth just for their own sakes are never satisfied and contented? They are always wanting something more and better. When a child of God practices giving, they are coming against that demon spirit with their resistance and are dealing it a deadly blow. Every gift is a reminder that God is their source and wealth has a greater purpose than for selfish gain.

There are people who are eaten up with materialism and it is sad. They never feel satisfied. It is almost like drinking all of the water you could drink but always feeling thirsty; eating all the food you could eat but always feeling hungry; sleeping all you could sleep but always being tired. That's the way materialism works. The more you get, the more you want. It's a deadly cycle.

People who tithe are able to fight that tendency and win victory. They learn the art of contentment. They are more satisfied because they understand the purpose of wealth. They are able to draw a context for their wealth and frame it with the Kingdom of God. Without that framework, wealth will bleed forever over the borders of reason looking for a place of completion and contentment. But it will never happen.

(6) People who give generously can't explain how it works.

They can't explain it. People who give will testify, like one of our elders did recently, that they live better on the 90% than they lived on 100%. Fred Fairrow was saved in our church. I baptized him in the YMCA pool. Since that time, he has completed our school of ministry and graduated from another Bible college with a degree. He has been an elder in our church for a couple of years now. He and his wife were both working adults when they got saved. When he first heard me talking about tithing, he wasn't sure how he and his wife were going to do it. They had never given away 10% of their income and tried to make it. If they were just getting by on the 100%, how could they ever survive on only 90%? Yet early on, Fred and Kathy decided to trust God's word and obey in faith. Recently they both confessed that somehow, they live better now without that 10% in their possession. How are they doing it? Fred said that he really can't explain it but it works!

In fact, all of our elders at church were saved as married adults with children. They were all in their mid to late thirties. Each one would testify of this miraculous truth. Along with the Fairrows, the Cucklers and Kings will tell you that if you give God what belongs to Him, He will bless the remaining 90% more than He could bless the 100%.

Another of our elders, Jim Cuckler, learned about tithing from listening to a preacher on the radio. When he got home that day from work he said, "Carol, we have got to start writing that tithe check BEFORE we write anything else." They have been doing that for over 30 years now! He recently testified during a church service to ways in which God blesses the tither:

> "Pastor Mark, when you said unexpected blessings come to the tither, I thought about this: We bought a car about two years ago, a Grand Marquis, 8-cylinder. It got about 21 miles a gallon. I checked it a couple of times. And according to the

way gas has been going up, in my head when we drive back and forth to Florida, I thought, well, it ought to run about $150 dollars. And I thought, you know, we're not spending that much, and I checked the mileage coming back and that car was getting 27 miles a gallon! And the only explanation I got for that was that God was making up for that high price of gas. I checked it twice and it gets 27 miles a gallon!"

God is ready for you to become a generous giver! He is ready to help you destroy the spirit of poverty that has kept you from fulfilling your destiny in Christ. I want you to walk in prosperity and become a supporter of the Lord's work worldwide. I want you to join the revolution that dreams bigger dreams, sees greater visions and puts poverty under our feet!

(7) People who give generously are laying up treasures in Heaven.

Jesus taught us to be aware of our heavenly treasures when He said in Matthew 6:19-20, "Do not lay up for yourselves treasures on earth, where moth and rust destroy and where thieves break in and steal but lay up for yourselves treasures in heaven, where neither moth nor rust destroys and where thieves do not break in and steal." People who give to the Lord's work on earth are laying up treasures in Heaven. One day, we are all going to be judged. Those who are born again and walk according to Biblical truths will be greatly rewarded in heaven. The saints who have preceded us would gladly testify to the fact that giving generously to the Lord on earth is well worth the investment!

CHAPTER 11

"Keeping the Accursed Thing"

Money is more than a coin or a piece of paper. The value of a dollar bill does not depend upon how much it costs to produce it but in what it represents. The exchange of money is more than making payroll and receiving a paycheck. Whenever two people enter into a working relationship, there is an exchange of power and influence for both parties. It is a trade-off. A paycheck is one man exchanging his power and influence for another man's power and influence. What makes the employer powerful and influential is his wealth. What makes the employee powerful and influential is his knowledge, energy and skill. Both parties need each other. Both are giving to the other a portion of their power and influence in exchange for further power and influence. When this exchange takes place, both sides are receiving more than money. They are taking legal ownership of the power and influence that has been given by the other person.

As we stated earlier in this book, the Jews and the Greeks thought differently. To a Greek, money is one-dimensional. He sees the dollar-bill with nothing more attached to it than the opportunity to own it and then spend it for something new. Any spiritual connection to that dollar-bill was separated from it and considered to be irrelevant. Westerners think like Greeks. We see money, make money, count money and value money with little or no spiritual considerations. Whether a person finds money on the sidewalk, wins it in a bingo game, gets it as a birthday gift, hits the lottery or makes it at work, it all spends the same. That's all we worry about.

To the Jewish mind, things were a little different. They saw the physical world and the spiritual world as inseparably intertwined, one affecting the other. They understood that activities in the spirit-world and activities in the physical world were taking place simultaneously in the same space and time. They understood that money meant more than what a person saw at face value. The Biblical writers understood that money could take on the spirit of the one who owned it.

If we were to take a coin or a dollar-bill and put it under a microscope, we could examine its physical properties. Under that microscope, however, you could not see demons, angels or any spiritual things. As Greek thinkers, we only consider those things that we can see or experience with the other four natural senses. Seeing things from a Biblical worldview, however, we would have to consider more than what could be seen with the natural eye. We might have to confess that certain physical objects can take on spiritual qualities. Money could, therefore, take on the spirit of its owner.

But how could this be? It seems almost ridiculous to say that money has a spirit, doesn't it? Answer me this: How did Jesus' clothes heal people? When the lady with the issue of blood touched the hem of His garment, how was the anointing taken from Him? When you read the passage you find that Jesus knew that life and power had left Him. How did that happen? That garment took on the anointing of the One who owned it and the lady who touched it in faith received spiritual power for healing.

Here's another question: How does the Holy Spirit get inside of you? A doctor can examine your physical body with no apparent evidence of the Holy Spirit. You are about nine buckets of water and one bucket of mud but somehow God has managed to put the Holy Spirit in you, didn't He? How do demons get inside of people? As Greek thinkers, we can examine the natural body without any evidence of spiritual influences. But the Bible makes it clear that the spirits of Satan can live within the physical bodies of those people who give themselves to him, taking on the spiritual qualities of the one who owns it.

Tell me how the handkerchief and apron of Paul healed the sick and cast out demons in Acts 19:12. It was just a piece of cloth. He may have purchased it at Wal-Mart but when they came into his possession and ownership, they began to change. If these items were put under a microscope, scientists would not be able to find any spiritual qualities. Yet the Bible says that these physical items had taken on a supernatural power from their owner to heal the sick and cast out demons. How did that happen?

How did the bones of Elisha, lying in the bottom of a grave, raise the dead? When some men put the dead body of their friend in Elisha's grave, the spiritual power of the man who owned those bones (Elisha) activated the life of the dead man and raised him up. Neither one of them was alive at the time. Neither one of them had faith for that miracle. How did that happen? I'll tell you how: Because the spirit-world and the physical world are not separated like we often suppose. They are inseparable and intermingled like mixed paint that has been blended together making a solid color. The bones of the prophet contained supernatural anointing in them that was physically experienced by the man who touched them.

Do you remember when Jesus was sold for 30 pieces of silver? Where did that money come from? It came as a bribe, a pay-off to Judas in exchange for the life of Jesus. When Judas saw what he had done, he took the 30 pieces of silver and threw them on the temple floor saying, "I don't want it." Later, he went out and hanged himself.

What did the officials of the temple do? They didn't pick up the money and put it in the church offering. They didn't pick up the money and go feed the poor with it. They didn't scoop up that money and put it in their pocket for lunch money the next day. "This is blood money," they said. "We don't want it." What they understood is what I want you to understand, that money takes on the spirit of the one who owns it. They knew that this money had taken on the spirit of Judas' betrayal. That money took on the murderous hatred of the Pharisees who originally hashed out the plan to murder Jesus. That money was full of hatred, deception, betrayal and murder.

The men who gathered it off the temple floor looked at one another and said, "This is blood money and we don't want it." So they took the money and bought a piece of ground near town and called it "The Field of Blood (Matthew 27:8)." Why did they do that? Because they understood that money takes on the spirit of the one who owns it and is affected by the conditions under which it was exchanged.

Does this make you wonder where your money has been? Was it used in a drug deal? Was it used as a payoff in mob hit? Was it used the night before in a strip club? Was it part of a child pornography purchase? Who knows? But here's the good part: God has provided a way to sanctify and cleanse it. Through giving of the tithe, He has provided a way for the entire 90% to be blessed! Do you want to redeem your money out of the world and bring it into the Kingdom of God? Then give the first ten percent to God and the rest will be blessed! It belongs to Him, anyway.

IS IT HOLY OR IS IT ACCURSED?

Leviticus 27:28 says, "Nevertheless no devoted offering that a man may devote (cherem) to the LORD of all that he has, both man and beast, or the field of his possession, shall be sold or redeemed; every devoted offering (cherem) is most holy to the LORD." There is an interesting Hebrew word that is used in this verse that is translated, "devoted." It is the word cherem. This word describes something that is holy and belongs to the Lord. But it also has a different meaning. This same Hebrew word is also translated, "accursed." In Joshua 7:1 it says, "But the children of Israel committed a trespass regarding the accursed things (cherem), for Achan...took of the accursed things (cherem); so the anger of the LORD burned against the children of Israel."

How could something be both holy and accursed at the same time? Here's how: By its owner! When God has His stuff in His hand it is holy but when we have God's stuff in our hand, it is accursed. The spoil from the first city taken under Joshua's invasion of Canaan belonged to the Lord. According to the principle of the firstfruits, if Israel would give to the Lord what belonged to Him, then the rest of the spoils of war would be blessed. God wanted them blessed. God wanted them prosperous. So He provided a plan that would destroy the spirit of poverty and release abundance on His children. All they were required to do was give the first part to Him. But when some of the devoted things ended up in Achan's possession, they became accursed. Therefore, what is holy can be accursed depending upon whose hands it is in.

When you hold onto God's ten percent, it is accursed in your hands. When you give it to Him, it becomes a blessed thing and ALL

Keeping the Accursed Thing

of what you own is blessed. Isn't that cool? If you want to know how to bring a blessing on all your money, read about Joshua and the children of Israel. If you want to get the spirit of the world off of your stuff, give to God what belongs to Him. If you want to walk under a curse, however, keep what belongs to Him and put yourself in Achan's shoes.

Israel came to Jericho and the walls miraculously came down. All of the spoils of the city were to be given to the Lord's work in the tabernacle. In giving to the work of the Lord, a person is giving to the Lord, Himself. However, unbeknownst to any of the leaders, a man named Achan took some of the spoil for himself and hid it in his tent.

The next town on the list was Ai. It was a small town that seemed like a cakewalk compared to Jericho. However, when Israel came against the city, they were soundly defeated. How did this happen? Joshua was at a loss. They had been promised victory and now they are suffering defeat. This is where the spirit of poverty jumps on a person. Remember, that spirit wants to steal your dreams and visions. It convinces people of their lack and tells them that they will never measure up. They will never walk in abundance. They will never walk in increase and prosperity.

Depressed, despondent and in despair, Joshua threw himself down on the ground in his tent and cried out to God. His prayer was not one of faith but of fear. Joshua knew that God's will for His people was victory and not defeat; advancement and not retreat; increase and not decrease, but he was having trouble reconciling why they had been so soundly defeated after their great victory at Jericho. It was then that God told Joshua these words:

> "Israel has sinned, and they have also transgressed My covenant which I commanded them. For they have even taken

some of the accursed things (cherem), and have both stolen and deceived; and they have also put it among their own stuff. Therefore the children of Israel could not stand before their enemies, but turned their backs before their enemies, because they had become doomed to destruction (cherem). Neither will I be with you anymore, unless you destroy the accursed (cherem) from among you. Get up, sanctify the people, and say, 'Sanctify yourselves for tomorrow, because thus says the LORD God of Israel: There is an accursed thing (cherem) in your midst, O Israel; you cannot stand before your enemies until you take away the accursed thing(cherem) from among you (Joshua 7:11-13).'"

God got his point across. Israel was defeated and doomed because they had kept God's stuff. The culprit was eventually found and dealt with appropriately. The moral of this story is simple. We need to give God what belongs to Him. If not, we will be defeated. It makes you wonder if the reason why so many churches and individual Christians are living in defeat isn't somehow connected with the fact that they are wearing an accursed thing, living in an accursed thing, driving an accursed thing, vacationing in an accursed thing, riding an accursed thing, sailing an accursed thing, etc. How can God bless a home that is keeping what belongs to him? How can God bless a church if choir members, deacons, ushers, elders and even senior pastors are robbing from Him and keeping His stuff? If we keep what belongs to God, it will become accursed. But if we give it to God, it becomes a holy thing and all of what we own is blessed!

PRAYING A PRAYER FOR PROSPERITY

Proverbs 3:9 says, "Honor the Lord with your possessions and with the first fruit of all your increase, so shall your barns be filled with plenty and your vats will overflow with new wine." We are told in this passage that we can honor the Lord with our possessions. If we are all poor, how can we do that? This verse assumes that the spirit of poverty is broken and the Lord's people are walking in prosperity and increase. If you want to walk under such a blessing, you must rid yourself of God's stuff, first. The accursed thing must become a holy thing in God's possession. When it is released from your ownership, it releases a blessing from heaven upon the rest of what you own.

God had a special confession for Israel about the tithe. He wanted them to have everything they owned blessed. In Deuteronomy 26:13-14 He taught them to say, "I have removed the holy tithe from my house, and also have given them to the Levite, the stranger, the fatherless, and the widow, according to all Your commandments which You have commanded me; I have not transgressed Your commandments, nor have I forgotten them. I have not eaten any of it when in mourning, nor have I removed any of it for an unclean use, nor given any of it for the dead. I have obeyed the voice of the LORD my God, and have done according to all that You have commanded me."

If you are still holding onto what belongs to God, I suggest you lay this book down and write that tithe check immediately. If you have to, make a special trip to your pastor's office and say, "Please take this! I have to get this out of my house before it becomes an accursed thing!" If he doesn't understand what you are talking to him about, give him a copy of this book!

Just after making that confession of not holding back on the tithe, Israel was supposed to pray a prayer like this: "Look down from Your holy habitation, from heaven, and bless Your people Israel and the land which You have given us, just as You swore to our fathers, a land flowing with milk and honey (Deuteronomy 26:15) ." Only a tither can pray that prayer right there. Only someone who has rid their home of the accursed thing can look up into heaven and pray for prosperity with a straight face. God wants you to be prosperous. God wants to defeat the spirit of poverty that attacks you. He wants to move you into a position of blessing. It all starts with honoring God with the first part of your increase. It belongs to Him. If you have done this, read that prayer again and begin praying it over your home, job, family, bank account, possessions, etc. Ask God to look down from heaven. Ask Him with confidence to bless your family and to bless the source of your prosperity (land). Remind him of His covenant promises that He swore to our fathers. And let Him know that you expect to live in a land flowing with milk and honey. You can expect this prayer to be answered because you have surrendered the accursed thing and made it, and everything else you own, a holy and blessed thing.

CONCLUSION

I want to call your attention to something that I wrote in the Author's Foreword of this book. I said that there was something that I learned since that cold, snowy night in 1999 when God stirred our hearts: Don't wait until a convenient time to obey the Lord - obey Him immediately! Right now, you may be stirred to cry out, "Deliver me, Lord!" You may want to break the spirit of poverty over your family, church and city. I want to encourage you not to wait another minute before doing so. Start thinking differently about yourself and your future today. Start thinking differently about the purpose of your wealth. Call your friends and family and start distributing copies of this book to them. Call your pastor and make plans to bless the ministries of your church and plan how to create more wealth. Begin creating prayer cells for the purpose of praying specifically for the prosperity of your congregation and for the economy of your city. Ask God to give good jobs to people that have none; promotions for people who work in large companies; lucrative contracts to people in business. We need to pray for the transfer of wealth that the prophets spoke about and then ask God for strategies to make it happen.

Think long term. Start planting these ideas in the hearts and minds of young people. As they work themselves through high school, help them to believe in themselves. Tell them to dream big and don't allow them to drop out of school. Challenge them to go on to college and get their undergraduate degrees, masters degrees and doctors degrees. Challenge them to be the next generation of university professors, scientists, lawyers, Supreme Court judges, builders, architects, schoolteachers, pastors, politicians, business owners, movie producers and parents. Do everything you can to release a generational blessing upon them. We need people on the earth who are transfixed on the cross, consumed with the Kingdom of God and creating, generating and distributing wealth throughout the earth. With people like you, we can surely advance the message of the Kingdom of God around the world before the return of Jesus Christ! Amen!